Real Thai

Real Thai
The Best of Thailand's Regional Cooking

By Nancie McDermott

Illustrations by
Jennie Oppenheimer

CHRONICLE BOOKS
SAN FRANCISCO

This book is dedicated with love, respect and gratitude to my parents and to my teachers.

Library of Congress Cataloging-in-Publication Data

McDermott, Nancie.
    Real Thai : the best of Thailand's regional cooking/by Nancie McDermott ; illustrations by Jennie Oppenheimer.
        p.   cm.
    Includes index.
    ISBN 0-8118-0017-2
    1. Cookery, Thai. 2. Thailand--Social life and customs.
I. Title.
TX724.5.T5M34   1992
641.59593--dc20   91-39533
                                                                      CIP

Printed in U.S.A.

ISBN 0-8118-0017-2

Distributed in Canada by Raincoast Books, 8680 Cambie Street, Vancouver, B.C. V6P 6M9

10 9 8 7 6 5

Chronicle Books
275 Fifth Street
San Francisco, CA 94103

TABLE OF CONTENTS

INTRODUCTION

I first went to Thailand in 1975, to spend two years working as a Peace Corps volunteer. My assignment was to teach English as a second language in a secondary school in the small town of Thatoom, on the Moon River in Surin Province. Surin, which borders on Cambodia, is about 360 miles from Bangkok, in the northeastern region of Thailand known as Pahk Issahn.

The students were eighth and ninth graders at Thatoom Prachasermwit, a comprehensive school participating in a World Bank program designed to increase educational opportunities in rural communities. I arrived in Thailand in April, but before I could begin teaching others, I went through three months of training that included practice teaching and intensive instruction in the beautiful, baffling tonal language of Thailand. Thirty of us lived in up-country hotels, first in the central Thai city of Nakorn Sawahn and later in the northernmost province of Chiang Rai.

Our days were spent in classrooms, and our evenings were devoted to language tutoring and CCT–cross-cultural training–a valiant effort on the part of our American and Thai training staff to acquaint us with Thai life. It touched on everything from politics and religion to table manners and how to sing a Thai song. April is the pinnacle of summertime in Thailand, and the heat was astounding, even for me, a veteran of twenty-three humid North Carolina summers. Frequent cold showers, a fresh dusting of baby powder, and a change of clothes gave a little relief, but a better remedy was a succession of very cold drinks. Small cafes near the hotel introduced me to Thai iced coffee and tea, concoctions so sweet, strong, and cold that I gladly lingered over the damp glass. In the evening, groups of us strolled to the night market in search of heavenly banana smoothies called *gluay bahn.*

Back home in North Carolina I had been raised to believe that there were times when it was just too hot to eat, but Thais have no such silly notions. They know it's always time to eat, and they take tremedous pleasure in fixing or finding the perfect treat for a given moment. Despite the soaring mercury, I eagerly expanded the repertoire of dishes I could pronounce well enough to order. First it was *kao paht,* fried rice seasoned with a squeeze of fresh lime. Then *kwaytiow,* soft, fresh rice noodles, a verbal challenge but worth mastering for the wealth of delicious ways the noodles are prepared. There is *kwaytiow paht si-yu,* stir-fried with beef, soy sauce, Chinese broccoli, and egg; *kwaytiow laht nah,* smothered in a delicious Cantonese-style gravy with beef, Chinese broccoli, and brown bean sauce; and best of all, *kwaytiow paht Thai,* stir-fried Thai style with garlic, tamarind, peanuts and chilies and served with cool, crunchy bean sprouts and a chunks of lime.

Kwaytiow nahm, meatballs with fat rice noodles in chicken soup, was my lesson in acquired tastes. Thai cooks toss in a handful of fresh cilantro just before serving, so that the aroma and flavor of this distinctive herb permeate the dish. Although I prided myself on being a brave and adventurous diner, I didn't like cilantro at all, and along with a few others timid eaters, sheepishly requested instruction in how to convey "Hold the cilantro!" to a Thai noodle chef. *Mai sai pahk chee!* our saintly language instructors taught us, convinced that we were indeed insane. And that is what I said for months, until little by little I began to like cilantro, and long after language training was over, found myself using a new phrase– *Sai pahk chee yuh-yaeh!* "Make mine heavy on the cilantro!"

By the time the three months of training were over and I went to my school in Surin, I had added dozens of dishes to my list and was beginning to understand a little about Thai food.

The cuisines of China and India are colorful threads woven into the tapestry of Thai cuisine. Chinese influence is quickly apparent in the vast numbers of noodle dishes beloved in Thailand, often unchanged from the way they are prepared in Chinese communities around the world. Noodles are a one-dish meal, especially popular for lunch and even breakfast, and they are about the only food that Thais do not share at the table. Doctoring one's plate of *paht Thai* or bowl of *kwaytiow nahm* is serious business for Thai diners, who have strong ideas about how much *krueng broong*, or "seasonings," to add. Fish sauce, chili-vinegar sauce, ground peanuts, sugar, lime, and crushed dried red chili are on every noodle-shop table, and I think I'm the only one who ever dug right into my plate of noodles, perfectly delighted with it the way it came. Thais first add two tablespoons of this and a bit of that, tossing everything until it suits their tastes. Noodle shops gave me my first intimation of how seriously these lighthearted people take food, not in a heavy, pedantic way, but in the sense of being devoted to getting the flavors just the way they like them to be.

Being of Chinese origin, noodles are also about the only food Thais eat with chopsticks. Most other dishes are enjoyed with a large spoon to catch the sauce and a fork in the other hand to help mix it in with the rice. Thais eat from the spoon, using the fork only for mixing and pushing bites of food onto the spoon.

Other Chinese legacies include extensive use of the techniques of stir-frying and steaming, although Thai stir-fries tend to be less complicated than their Chinese counterparts. In the Thai kitchen, there is little fuss over cutting ingredients to a precise size and shape, and cooks seldom marinate meat with seasonings or use cornstarch to thicken and glaze sauces. Chinese-style dishes that have a solid home in Thailand include *moo paht brow wahn*, pork with vegetables in sweet-sour sauce; *gai paht meht mamuang himapahn*, chicken with cashews; *moo phat king*, pork with mushrooms and fresh ginger; and *kao mun gai*, Hainan-style chicken and rice.

Thailand's Indian heritage is strongest in the brilliant use of spices and herbs. Thai curry pastes are descendants of the wet *masalas* of India, in which fresh herbs and roots are ground with dried toasted spices to create aromatic seasoning pastes. An affection for chilies, coconut milk, tamarind, ginger, and cilantro is shared between the two countries, as is the style of cooking rice so that it comes out in fluffy separate grains. Rice is always eaten from a plate, using either the right hand or a spoon, rather than from a rice bowl with chopsticks.

Thailand has five regions with distinct geographical and cultural differences. This book devotes a chapter to each region: the Center, the North, the South, the Northeast, and the Gulf Coast. These are followed by a chapter of basic recipes and a glossary.

Each regional chapter opens with an introduction to acquaint you with the land, its people, and the food that sustains them in their daily lives. The basic recipes chapter contains recipes for dishes used throughout the book: rice, curry pastes, sauces, and the techniques for making less familiar ingredients such as tamarind liquid, roasted rice powder, and fresh coconut milk. Many of these basic preparations can be purchased in Asian markets if you are short on time, so check the glossary for additional information.

The glossary defines many of the ingredients used in this book, so look there whenever you encounter an unfamiliar one, or simply want to know more about one you already use in your kitchen. It includes descriptions of each ingredient to help you recognize it in Asian markets and explains how it is used and stored. Each entry also lists other names by which these ingredients are widely known, and suggests substitutions for them whenever possible.

I have also transliterated the Thai recipe names and glossary items into the Latin alphabet to aid you in trying to remember and pronounce them. Spellings of transliterated Thai words vary wildly, as any reader of Thai restaurant menus in the West already knows. My goal here is to enable you to pronounce these Thai words well enough to be understood by Thai people. Since Thai is a tonal language, you will still be off the mark, but it's a good start and I hope it will earn you at the least a legendary heartwarming Thai smile.

Within each chapter I have arranged the recipes as nearly as possible in a standard Western menu order: appetizers and snacks; stir-fries, curries, soups, and other dishes that go with plain rice; one-dish meals such as noodles and rice dishes; and sweets. In Thailand, a variety of the dishes with rice would make up a full meal, with all the dishes served at once and shared. The appetizers, snacks, and sweets would be enjoyed throughout the day and evening, as a nibble between meals, or a treat at the night market on a sultry summer evening.

It is important to read through a recipe completely before you begin to prepare it. Notes to the cook follow many of the recipes and contain additional information about alternative techniques, ingredients, or presentation. When I say that a recipe serves a certain number of people, I am expecting that you will be serving it with one or more other dishes, as well as with lots of rice. Thais eat rice, and the other stuff goes with it: *entree* or *main dish* in Thai is in fact a phrase, *gahp kao,* which literally means "with rice." They love variety in their food as well as in life, and, rather than doubling a recipe, they prefer small amounts from a wide array of dishes.

In putting a menu together, a Thai cook seeks variety in cooking method, ingredients, textures, temperature, and flavor. If a curry, which is fiery hot with chilies and rich and sweet with coconut milk, anchors the menu, Thais will still want a soup. A clear Chinese-style soup would be a good choice, since the two most beloved Thai soups would be repetitious: shrimp and lemongrass soup would be redundantly fiery hot, and chicken coconut soup would be redundantly rich and sweet. If they order *mee grop,* which is crispy and sweet, they will still want a whole fish not a meaty fried fish with a sweet-sour sauce, but a Chinese-style steamed flounder, delicately flavored with ginger, garlic, and green onions.

Don't let this business of menu planning become a burden to you. What I am describing is a Thai way of thinking about food, and for them it comes effortlessly. If you find yourself worrying about whether you have enough variety or authenticity, slow down and dream up a way to make it fun. Try one Thai dish with a menu you already enjoy, or have an all finger-food meal just because you hate to wash dishes. Most important to me is that you catch the real Thai spirit of enjoying the moment and pleasing yourself. Then your food will be as exotically wonderful as the kingdom that inspired this book.

During my two years of teaching in Thatoom, Surin, I lived in a large, Thai-style wooden house a short walk from the school. Weekdays I had several students living with me, since their homes were too far away for them to travel back and forth each day. As is traditional in up-country Thailand, I provided room and board, while they helped me with chores and kept our kitchen supplied with rice from their families' yearly crops.

Our kitchen was typical of those in the Thai countryside. It was located beneath the house, which was elevated on posts with the living area upstairs. We had two small charcoal stoves, a few side tables, and two immense *ohng* jars made of glazed earthenware, one filled with drinking water and the other with rice. There was also a *thoo,* a big freestanding cupboard with small, oddly shaped ceramic cups encircling its legs. These were tiny moats, a simple but effective means of barring tenacious ants from tiptoeing up to raid the prepared foods and condiments stored in the *thoo.* The tables held our *batterie de cuisine*—the cutting board, a hefty circle of tamarind wood a foot wide; several mighty cleavers and an array of paring knives; two large mortars with pestles, one Lao style, deep enough for pounding green papaya salad, and the other Thai style, squat and heavy for grinding and pounding curry pastes; *maw gaeng,* soup and curry pots of assorted sizes; a wok; and an array of long handled spoons, sieves, and scrapers for stir-frying and deep-frying.

We didn't have a special steamer—my students simply crossed two chopsticks in the wok and placed plates and bowls on top of them when we wanted *kai toon* (savory egg custard) or *haw moke* (fish in banana leaf packets). We also managed without a refrigerator, since I loved the Thai habit of daily trips to the fresh market and enjoyed this chore almost every morning. It's a habit I fell into of necessity and have continued in the years since for the pleasure it brings me. Even with a huge refrigerator and a car with a trunk that could hold a week's worth of groceries, I still like to *bai tahlaht,* or "go to the market," every day or two, and I dawdle and wander even in the wide, organized aisles of American grocery stores.

All you'll need in terms of equipment to cook the Thai dishes in this book are a cutting board and cleaver, paring knives, a wok, and several sizes of saucepans with tight-fitting lids. To make curry pastes, you'll also need a large, heavy mortar and pestle made of granite or clay. Even if you don't have all of these items, you can still make great Thai food.

Knives are such a help in cooking that I hope you treat yourself to excellent cutlery, despite the fact that the prices can be steep. Think of it as an investment rather than a luxury, and find a teacher to help you if you don't feel comfortable with basic knife skills. A large chef's knife can do most of the work of a Chinese cleaver, and a little paring knife can handle the small jobs. Remember to store them carefully and to keep them sharp.

I find a wok so useful that I couldn't do without mine, but almost all the dishes in this book can be cooked in a large, deep skillet. I'm particularly fond of using electric woks for deep-frying and steaming; they have steady bases and can be set up as a separate "station" in a corner of the kitchen, leaving the stove top free for the other cooking.

If you find yourself learning to love rice as much as I have, treat yourself to an electric rice cooker. It's a respected modern addition to every Thai kitchen I've been in save those without electricity. It does the job well and frees your stove top as well as your attention for other cook's tasks.

Instead of a mortar and pestle, you can use a spice grinder to turn roasted spices and rice grains into fragrant powder, and a blender or food processor with a small container or work bowl for turning fresh moist herbs and ground spices into flavorful curry pastes. You can also buy ground spices and add them to herbs in a blender, or simply buy prepared curry pastes, as many busy Thai cooks do.

Time is an issue for Thai cooks as well as for cooks in the West, whether they're pedaling a bicycle to the up-country market or hopping in the car for a run to a *soo-pah*—the "supermarket." Whatever improvisations and shortcuts you can devise to make cooking these dishes easy and fun will be very much in the authentic spirit of Thailand, an enchanting country brilliantly aware of the wisdom of enjoying life in each magnificent present moment.

PAHK KLAHNG
The Center

Central Thailand is a vast, fertile checkerboard of rice fields and orchards, finely veined with rivers and a network of canals. The cooks of this prosperous region have always had an abundance of glorious raw materials to inspire them, and they use a playful hand to turn the bounty of their fields, gardens, and waterways into unique, delicious food.

Central Thai dishes fall into two main categories that have evolved over time. Palace cooking is a cuisine of elaborate dishes created for the pleasure of royalty and nobility, while traditional home cooking is Thai food with a simple, practical focus.

Presentation is extremely important in palace-style cuisine, where chefs may spend as much time arranging the garnishes of a dish as they did in preparing it. Vegetable and fruit carving are respected Thai household arts that have been practiced for centuries. Expert artisans create stunning and beautiful displays of flowers and other objects carved from ginger, carrots, pumpkins, watermelons, and other vegetables and fruits.

But in the everyday Thai kitchen, no one has time to turn a pineapple into a boat or spiral a tomato skin into a perfect rose. Cooks cook and work at making things taste delicious, and if there's cilantro handy, a flourish of leaves may adorn the finished product as it is served up. What Thais care most about is great cooking, and they expect and enjoy fancy presentations in their place, at banquets, in fine restaurants, and on special occasions.

Mee grop, the epitome of palace cuisine, is a spectacular construction of rice noodles crisp fried until they puff, tossed with shrimp in a sweet-sour sauce, crowned with lacy egg nets, and garnished with green onion brushes, red chili flowers, and a confetti of pickled garlic, bean sprouts, and garlic chives. Preparation of this dish is so time-consuming that it's seldom served in restaurants in Thailand. There cooks prepare it for wedding banquets and other grand celebrations, when there will be lots of helping hands and good company to share the considerable effort.

Paht Thai is the home-style version of the same dish without the glamorous presentation, although it's more likely to be served in noodle cafes than prepared at home. The bean sprout garnish is still there, because, plain or fancy, Thais want that cool, crisp contrast to hot, sharp noodles.

Additional home-style dishes include *gai paht bai graprao,* a quick stir-fry of minced chicken with lots of garlic and chilies and a peppery flourish of holy basil; *kai toon,* a velvety steamed custard topped with golden bits of fried garlic in oil; *gradook moo tote,* tiny, tasty spareribs flavored with garlic, cilantro root, and pepper; and *yum kai kem,* a simple salad of salty eggs with chilies, shallots, and a squeeze of lime.

Palace-style dishes tend to be sweeter and less hot, and they use coconut milk more often, since there are always enough kitchen helpers to handle the labor-intensive task of extracting the milk. Among the palace-style favorites are *mah haw,* precious bites of savory minced pork on fresh pineapple; *kai yaht sai,* omelets stuffed with a salty-sweet pork filling, folded into appealing packets, and garnished with cilantro and red chilies; and *kanome jeen sao nahm,* nests of freshly made rice noodles topped with fresh ginger, salty dried shrimp, garlic, and slivers of pineapple, and served with a salty-sweet coconut sauce.

Whether you're in the mood to create a culinary masterpiece worthy of royalty, or just hungry for some good home cooking, the traditional cuisine of central Thailand is a bountiful resource.

BOH BIAH TOTE
Fried Spring Rolls

These savory packets are popular street food throughout Southeast Asia. Thais wrap a garlicky pork and noodle filling in delicate pancakes made of flour and water. The spring rolls fry up light and crisp, and are served with a dipping sauce of chili and garlic, a piquant sweet-sour partner for this delicious finger food. Since they're some trouble to make, consider preparing the filling and dipping sauce a day ahead and bribing guests to arrive early to help with the rolling and cooking.

2 packets (2 ounces each) bean thread noodles
1 tablespoon tiny dried cloud ears
Vegetable oil for sautéing and deep-frying
2 eggs, lightly beaten
Sweet-Hot Garlic Sauce (page 189)
2 tablespoons fish sauce
1 teaspoon freshly ground pepper
1 teaspoon sugar
1 tablespoon coarsely chopped garlic
1/4 cup finely chopped shallot or onion
1/2 pound ground pork
1/2 pound shrimp, peeled, deveined, and coarsely chopped
1 package (1 pound) spring roll wrappers
A handful of fresh cilantro leaves

Place the bean thread noodles in a large bowl, cover with warm water, and soak until softened, about 30 minutes. Place cloud ears in a medium bowl, cover with warm water, and soak until softened, about 30 minutes.

Meanwhile, coat a small skillet with a little oil and warm for 1 minute over medium heat. Pour in one fourth of the eggs, tip the pan so that the egg covers the bottom in a thin sheet, and cook until set and opaque, less than 1 minute. Turn the egg sheet out onto a plate and repeat with the remaining eggs in 3 batches. When the sheets are cool, stack and slice into long, thin shreds. Set the shreds aside in a large bowl.

Make the Sweet-Hot Garlic Sauce (page 189) and set aside to cool to room temperature.

Drain the noodles well and dump the tangle onto a cutting board. Shape the noodles into a log and cut into 2-inch lengths. Precision doesn't count here—you're just trying to make them a little more manageable for stir-frying. Add the noodles to the bowl containing the egg shreds.

Drain the cloud ears and place on a cutting board. Check them over with your fingers, cutting off and discarding any hard little navels you may find. Slice the cloud ears into long, thin shreds. Add them to the bowl containing the noodles and egg shreds and set it aside near the stove. Combine the fish sauce, pepper, and sugar in a small bowl and place it next to the stove along with the garlic, shallot, pork, and shrimp.

Heat a wok or medium skillet over medium-high heat. Add 1 tablespoon oil and swirl to coat the surface. When the oil is very hot, add the garlic and stir-fry until golden, about 15 seconds. Add the shallot and stir-fry until wilted. Add the pork and stir-fry until no longer pink, about 2 minutes. Add the shrimp and stir-fry until pink and opaque, about 1 minute. Add the fish sauce mixture and toss well.

Add the noodles, cloud ears, and egg strips and stir-fry, tumbling and turning all the ingredients over and over, for 1 to 2 minutes. Notice how the noodles change from stiff, white, and wiry to clear, soft, and curly. As soon as they've transformed and all the ingredients are well combined, turn the filling out into a large bowl and let cool to room temperature.

Gently separate the spring roll wrappers. Place 1 wrapper, smooth side down, on a work surface; cover the remaining wrappers with a dampened paper towel while you work. Position the wrapper with a point toward you. Place a heaping spoonful of the filling in the center of the half of the diamond that's closest to you. Use your fingers to shape the filling into a log about 3 inches long. Fold the wrapper point closest to you up, over, and around the filling. Begin to roll the wrapper and, when you've rolled halfway to the top point, fold the right and left sides in toward the middle. Then keep rolling. When you reach the top point, moisten it with water and seal the roll like an envelope. Set the roll aside on a tray or baking sheet with the seam side down.

Continue rolling until you've used up all the filling, spacing finished rolls so that they don't touch each other and separating successive layers with plastic wrap.

Pour the oil into a wok or a deep, wide saucepan to a depth of 3 inches. Heat over medium heat to 350° to 375°F. Meanwhile, prepare a drain basket for the fried spring rolls by lining a colander or large strainer with paper towels, with something under it to catch any drips. Drop a tiny piece of wrapper into the wok. If it sizzles immediately, the oil is ready.

Carefully add a spring roll by sliding it gently down the curved side of the wok and into the oil, where it should sizzle and bubble at once. Add 2 more spring rolls and cook 3 at a time, turning occasionally and frying until golden brown, about 3 minutes.

Remove the spring rolls with a long-handled mesh scoop or slotted spoon, hold them over the oil to drain for a few moments, and transfer to the prepared colander or strainer to drain. Place the spring rolls on a serving platter, garnish with the cilantro, and serve with small saucers of the dipping sauce.

MAKES ABOUT 32 SPRING ROLLS.

MAH HAW
Savory Minced Pork on Pineapple

For *mah haw*, small squares of fresh pineapple are crowned with a salty-sweet mix of pork, palm sugar, and peanuts, and garnished with cilantro leaves and sweet red pepper.

The Thai name of this dish is one of those enigmatic Oriental mysteries. It's translated as "galloping horses," yet the literal meaning is "horses of the Haw people." The Haw are a tribal group from the southwestern Chinese province of Yunnan who migrated into northern Thailand long ago. This dish has none of the hallmarks of a food on which migrating tribal people survive, so I'm stumped.

1 teaspoon vegetable oil
3 tablespoons Cilantro Pesto (page 168)
1/2 pound coarsely ground pork
2 tablespoons fish sauce
2 tablespoons palm sugar or brown sugar
1 small to medium pineapple
2 fresh red chee fah *chilies, cut into long, thin strips, or 6 long, thin sweet red pepper strips*
A handful of small fresh cilantro leaves

Heat a wok or medium skillet over medium heat. Add the oil, and swirl to coat the surface. When the oil is hot, add the herb paste. Stir-fry the paste until quite fragrant, about 2 minutes. Increase the heat to medium high and crumble in the ground pork. Stir-fry the pork until it breaks up into small lumps, renders some of its fat, and is no longer pink, about 2 minutes.

Add the fish sauce and sugar and continue cooking, stirring and scraping often to brown and coat the meat evenly. After about 4 minutes, when the meat is nicely browned, remove the pan from the heat and taste the sauce for a pleasing salty-sweet balance. Add more fish sauce and palm sugar if needed and return to the heat to reduce the additions. Remove from the heat, transfer to a medium bowl, and let cool to room temperature.

Peel the pineapple and cut crosswise into 1/4-inch-thick slices. Remove the hard core from the center of each slice and cut the slices into 1-inch squares. You should have about 2 cups of squares.

To serve, mound a spoonful of savory pork onto each pineapple square. Garnish each mound with chili strips and cilantro leaves. Transfer to a beautiful platter and serve at room temperature as finger food.

SERVES 10 TO 12.

GAI SAHM YAHNG
Three Kinds of Chicken

The name of this tasty snack is a mystery, since there's no chicken in it. But it's an easy dish to fix and great with beer, wine, or sparkling cider. So invite your friends over to sip and munch while they help you ponder the curious name.

2 stalks fresh lemongrass
3 tablespoons diced, peeled fresh ginger
3 tablespoons coarsely chopped shallot
1/2 cup tiny dried shrimp
1/2 cup salted, dry-roasted peanuts or cashews

Trim the lemongrass, cutting away and discarding the grassy tops to leave only 2 inches of the bulb end; cut away any hard root section to form a clean, smooth, flat base on each bulb. Remove and discard tough outer leaves. Slice the lemongrass crosswise into very thin circles.

Place the lemongrass in a mound on a small serving plate. Arrange all the other ingredients in separate small piles on the same plate. Each guest picks up a bit of each ingredient to make a small mouthful.

SERVES 4.

GRADOOK MOO TOTE
Pork Spareribs with Cilantro and Garlic

> *Gradook moo tote* is a habit-forming Thai version of Chinese spareribs. These gloriously garlicky ribs are tastiest after they have cooled for 5 to 10 minutes.

2 pounds pork spareribs, cut into 1-inch lengths (see Note)
3 tablespoons Cilantro Pesto (page 168)
3 tablespoons fish sauce
1 teaspoon sugar
Vegetable oil for deep-frying
A handful of fresh cilantro leaves

Combine the spareribs, Cilantro Pesto, fish sauce, and sugar in a large mixing bowl. Toss to coat the spareribs evenly. Cover tightly and refrigerate for 30 minutes to 1 hour.

Pour the oil into a wok or a deep, wide saucepan to a depth of 3 inches. Heat over medium heat to 350° to 375°F. While the oil is heating, line a large plate or tray with paper towels for draining the cooked ribs and select an attractive serving platter. Have a long-handled, mesh scoop or a slotted spoon alongside the wok to use for removing the cooked ribs.

When the oil is hot, carefully add about one third of the spareribs. The oil should sizzle and foam as they begin to brown and cook. Stir gently to separate the ribs and help them brown evenly. Let them cook until the meat is nicely browned and cooked through at the thickest part, 4 to 6 minutes. As soon as they're done, remove them from the oil with the scoop and drain them on the paper towel–lined plate. Cook the remaining 2 batches in the same manner.

Arrange the cooked ribs on the serving platter and garnish with the cilantro. Serve warm. Provide a bowl for the leftover bones.

SERVES 4 TO 6.

NOTE: To prepare these spareribs Thai style, you'll need small pieces, about 1 inch long. Have the butcher cut the slab of spareribs across the bones into 1-inch lengths. Then you can cut the ribs lengthwise between the bones into small pieces. You can also use long spareribs with delicious results.

MEHT MAMUANG HIMAPAHN TOTE
Fried Cashews

Golden fried cashews are perfect with a tall Thai limeade or a frosty Singha beer. The fried whole chilies are for those who love super-hot food.

Peanut oil or other vegetable oil for frying
1/2 pound raw whole cashews
1/2 cup small dried red chilies
1 teaspoon salt
3 tablespoons thinly sliced green onions (sliced crosswise)

Line a large mixing bowl with paper towels and place it by the stove, along with a long-handled mesh scoop or a slotted spoon. Pour the oil into a wok or large, deep skillet to a depth of about 3 inches. Heat over medium-low heat until fairly hot, 300° to 325°F. This will take about 10 minutes. Add the cashews to the oil and stir gently. Fry for about 5 minutes, lifting them out of the oil now and then with the scoop and continuing to stir gently.

When the nuts are a rich, reddish gold, scoop them out of the oil, holding them over the wok to drain for about 30 seconds and shaking the scoop a little, then drop them into the mixing bowl.

Place the whole chilies in the scoop and lower them into the oil for about 30 seconds, then pull them out. Repeat, dipping the chilies in and out for short baths until they darken a little and smell rich and roasted. If they burn, discard them and start again with a new batch of chilies. When the chilies are done, turn off the heat and drain them over the pan, then set them aside on a plate.

Transfer the cashews, which should still be hot, to another bowl and sprinkle with the salt. Shake and toss to season evenly. Let cool for about 5 minutes and transfer to a serving plate. Place the fried chilies alongside the nuts and sprinkle the green onions over the top. Serve at once.

SERVES 4.

LONE DAO JIOW
Dao Jiow-Coconut Sauce with Fresh Vegetables

> *Lone dao jiow* is a type of *nahm prik*, a strong-flavored sauce served with an array of fresh vegetables and a plate of rice. *Lones* are richer than other *nahm priks* because they have coconut milk as a base and often include pork or fresh shrimp rather than salted fish or dried shrimp. This *lone* is made with *dao jiow*, the extremely salty fermented soybeans beloved by Thais. Small spoonfuls of *dao jiow* add a punch to vegetable stir-fries and noodle dishes such as *paht Thai* (page 51) and *mee grop* (page 58), but there they play in the chorus, providing an indistinct background flavor. Here they take the starring role in a classic Thai harmony of salty, sour, and sweet.

1 cup coconut milk
1/3 cup brown bean sauce (dao jiow)
3 tablespoons thinly sliced shallot (sliced lengthwise)
1/4 pound pork, finely minced
1/4 pound shrimp, peeled, deveined, and finely minced
2 tablespoons palm sugar or brown sugar
2 tablespoons Tamarind Liquid (page 185)
3 small cucumbers, peeled and sliced on the diagonal into thick ovals
3 wedges green cabbage (about 2 inches wide at widest point)
6 green beans, trimmed

In a small, heavy-bottomed saucepan, bring the coconut milk to a gentle simmer over low heat. Cook, stirring gently now and then, until the coconut milk is fragrant and its oil glistens on the surface, 6 to 8 minutes.

While the coconut milk simmers, combine the bean sauce and 1 1/2 tablespoons of the shallot in a mortar. Using a pestle, mash the mixture to a chunky paste.

When the coconut milk is ready, add the shallot paste and stir well. Crumble in the pork and shrimp and simmer until the meat is cooked, 5 minutes.

Stir in the remaining 1 1/2 tablespoons shallot and sugar and simmer until the shallot wilts and the sugar melts, 1 or 2 minutes. Add the tamarind and taste the sauce, which should be a pleasing balance of salty, sour, and sweet. Adjust to your liking and remove from the heat.

Transfer the sauce to a small bowl and place it on a platter with the cucumbers, cabbage wedges, and green beans. Serve warm or at room temperature.

SERVES 4.

NOTE: If you don't have a mortar and pestle, finely chop the shallots and use a fork to mash them with the bean sauce to make a coarse paste.

GAENG KIOW WAHN GAI
Green Chicken Curry

Green curries take their name from the fierce, green *kii noo* chilies that are the base of the curry paste. It's a wonderful blend and my favorite Thai curry.

Kanome jeen, a soft, white rice noodle folded into little nests and sold in every Thai market, is a popular accompaniment to green curry. You can serve it with any type of cooked noodles, however. Prepare the noodles, place them in individual serving bowls while the curry heats, and add the curry just before serving. Steamed rice is also a good accompaniment.

1 whole chicken breast
2 chicken thighs
1/2 cup coconut cream
1/4 cup Green Curry Paste (page 169)
3 cups coconut milk
1 1/2 cups diced eggplant (1-inch dice)
2 tablespoons fish sauce
1 tablespoon palm sugar or brown sugar
1/2 teaspoon salt
12 fresh wild lime leaves
1/2 cup horapah basil leaves or other fresh basil leaves
3 fresh red chee fah chilies, sliced on the diagonal into ovals about 1/2 inch thick,
or 9 long, thin sweet red pepper strips

Bone and skin the chicken breast and thighs. You should have about 1 pound of meat. Cut the meat into large, bite-sized pieces; set aside.

In a medium, heavy-bottomed saucepan, warm the coconut cream over medium heat until it boils gently. Adjust the heat to maintain a gentle boil and cook for 6 to 8 minutes, stirring occasionally. The coconut cream will become fragrant as it thickens. When you see tiny pools of oil glistening on the surface, add the curry paste and stir to dissolve it into the coconut cream. Continue cooking for 1 to 2 minutes, until the curry paste has a pleasing aroma.

Add the chicken pieces and stir-fry for 1 to 2 minutes to coat them evenly with the paste. Cook for about 2 minutes. Increase the heat and add the coconut milk, eggplant, fish sauce, sugar, and salt; stir well. Stir in 6 of the lime leaves, adjust the heat to maintain a gentle, active boil and cook for 8 to 10 minutes, stirring occasionally. Taste and adjust the seasoning with a little more fish sauce, sugar, or curry paste.

When the chicken is done and the eggplant is just tender, remove from the heat and transfer to a serving bowl. Scatter the basil leaves, chilies, and the remaining 6 lime leaves on top and serve hot or warm.

SERVES 6.

NOTE: To cook the curry in advance, prepare it up to the point where it has been cooked with the lime leaves, except do not add the eggplant. Cool to room temperature, cover, and refrigerate for up to 24 hours. To serve, bring the curry back to a gentle boil over medium heat. Add the eggplant and proceed as directed.

Thais use the golfball-sized eggplants called *makeua poh,* often labeled Thai eggplants in Asian stores here. If you use this type, stem and quarter them lengthwise instead of dicing them. They may need a little more time to become tender than other types of eggplant. Thai cooks also add a handful of *makeua peuang,* a tiny eggplant that grows in clusters and resembles a large, hard green pea. There's no substitute, but the curry is still delicious without them.

If you can find neither the red chilies nor the sweet red pepper, omit them.

Chicken is used in the classic green curry, but Thais like it with beef as well. I like to make green curry with shrimp or seafood and snow peas instead of eggplant, adding them both at the end when the curry is done and cooking them just until they are tender.

GAENG PEHT NEUA
Red Beef Curry

Peht means "spicy hot," and this curry, made with a paste of dried red chilies, should be extremely hot. Red curry with chicken and bamboo is another popular combination, but use your imagination to come up with your own favorite red curry dish. Steamed rice is a good foil for this fiery dish.

1/2 cup coconut cream
1/4 cup Red Curry Paste (page 171)
1 pound lean beef, thinly sliced into strips 2 inches by 1 inch
3 cups coconut milk
About 2 pounds kabocha *pumpkin or any hard winter squash, peeled and cut into bite-sized chunks (1 1/2 cups)*
2 tablespoons fish sauce
1 tablespoon palm sugar or brown sugar
1/2 teaspoon salt
1/2 cup fresh horapah *basil leaves or other fresh basil leaves*

In a medium, heavy-bottomed saucepan, warm the coconut cream over medium heat until it boils gently. Adjust the heat to maintain a gentle boil and cook for 6 to 8 minutes, stirring occasionally. The coconut cream will become fragrant as it thickens. When you see tiny pools of oil glistening on the surface, add the curry paste and stir to dissolve it into the coconut cream. Continue cooking for 1 to 2 minutes, until the curry paste has a pleasing aroma.

Add the beef and stir-fry to coat it evenly with the paste. Cook for 2 minutes. Increase the heat and add the coconut milk, pumpkin, fish sauce, sugar, and salt; stir well. Adjust the heat to maintain a gentle, active boil and cook for 8 to 10 minutes, stirring occasionally. Taste and adjust the seasoning with a little more fish sauce, sugar, or curry paste.

When the beef is done and the pumpkin is just tender, stir in 1/4 cup of the basil leaves. Remove from the heat and transfer to a serving bowl. Scatter the remaining 1/4 cup basil leaves on top and serve hot or warm.

SERVES 6.

NOTE: To cook the curry in advance, prepare it up to the point where the basil is stirred in. Cool to room temperature, cover, and refrigerate for up to 24 hours. To serve, bring the curry back to a gentle boil over medium heat. Stir in the basil and proceed as directed.

Chunks of sweet potato or eggplant can be substituted for the pumpkin. You could also use chunks of zucchini or yellow squash, adding them about 3 minutes before the basil.

GAENG PEHT BEHT YAHNG
Chinese Roast Duck in Red Curry

This curry is a Thai marriage of two rich and luxurious foods: succulent, Chinese-style roast duck and creamy coconut milk. Pineapple chunks or cherry tomatoes provide a counterpoint of sharp, clear flavor, and, like all curries, the dish calls for lots of rice. I buy a whole roast duck at a Chinese barbecue restaurant, where they chop it up into serving pieces. I serve half of it with its warm crispy skin and dark, slightly sweet juices. I bone and refrigerate the other half to use in this curry, which tastes best if you make it in advance, chill it, and reheat it just before serving.

1/2 cup coconut cream
2 tablespoons Red Curry Paste (page 171)
2 cups chopped, boned Chinese-style roast duck (2-inch chunks)
3 cups coconut milk
1/2 small pineapple, peeled and cut into bite-sized chunks (about 1 cup) or 1 cup
  cherry tomatoes
1 tablespoon fish sauce
1 tablespoon palm sugar or brown sugar
12 fresh wild lime leaves
A handful of fresh horapah basil leaves or other fresh basil leaves

In a medium, heavy-bottomed saucepan, warm the coconut cream over medium heat until it boils gently. Adjust the heat to maintain a gentle boil and cook for 6 to 8 minutes, stirring occasionally. The coconut cream will become fragrant as it thickens. When you see tiny pools of oil glistening on the surface, add the curry paste and stir to dissolve it into the coconut cream. Continue cooking for 1 to 2 minutes, until the curry paste has a pleasing aroma.

Add the duck and stir-fry to coat it evenly with the paste. Cook for 1 to 2 minutes. Increase the heat and add the coconut milk, pineapple, fish sauce, sugar, and 6 of the lime leaves. Adjust the heat to maintain a gentle simmer and cook for 6 to 8 minutes, stirring once or twice. Taste and adjust the seasoning with fish sauce or sugar. Remove from the heat, let cool to room temperature, then cover and chill a few hours or overnight.

To serve, discard some of the fat from the surface of the curry, and warm the curry gently, uncovered, over low heat, until just hot but not boiling. Remove from the heat and transfer to a serving bowl. Stir in the basil leaves and the remaining 6 lime leaves and serve hot or warm.

SERVES 4 TO 6.

CHOO CHEE GOONG
Choo Chee Shrimp

Choo chee dishes are thick, rich fish and seafood curries, made with smaller than usual amounts of coconut milk and lots of pungent herbs. The traditional curry paste for *choo chee* curries is *krueng gaeng kua*, a red curry paste made without the toasted cumin, coriander seed, and peppercorns that are used in most other curries. But any red curry paste will work just fine.

This elegant dish is quick and easy to make. Serve it with jasmine rice and a simple salad or a stir-fried vegetable such as Spinach Sautéed with Garlic (page 38). I like to make this curry in advance, reserving the raw shrimp and the fresh herbs to add at the last minute when it is reheated and ready to serve.

1/2 cup coconut cream
1 heaping tablespoon Red Curry Paste (page 171)
1 cup coconut milk
1 tablespoon fish sauce
1 tablespoon palm sugar or brown sugar
3/4 pound medium to large shrimp, peeled, deveined, and halved lengthwise
1 handful of fresh horapah basil leaves or other fresh basil leaves
12 fresh wild lime leaves

In a medium heavy-bottomed saucepan, warm the coconut cream over medium heat until it boils gently. Adjust the heat to maintain a gentle boil and cook for 6 to 8 minutes, stirring occasionally. The coconut cream will become fragrant as it thickens. When you see tiny pools of oil glistening on the surface, add the curry paste and stir to dissolve the paste into the coconut cream. Continue cooking for 1 to 2 minutes.

Add the coconut milk, fish sauce, and sugar and stir well. Adjust heat to maintain a gentle, active boil and cook for 8 to10 minutes, stirring occasionally, until the curry is reduced and thickened. Taste and adjust the seasoning with a little more fish sauce, sugar, or curry paste. It should be very flavorful since it will be eaten with plain rice.

Add the shrimp, half of the basil leaves, and 6 of the lime leaves and stir to combine with the curry. Cook the shrimp until they curl and are cooked through, 1 to 2 minutes.

Remove from the heat, stir in the remaining basil and lime leaves, reserving a few leaves for arranging on top, and transfer to a serving dish. Scatter the reserved leaves on top and serve hot or warm.

SERVES 4.

NOTE: This dish traditionally calls for fresh leaves of *horapah* basil and the wild lime tree, but you could use any type of fresh basil and a tablespoon of lime zest if you don't have these fresh herbs handy. Even if you omit them altogether, you will still have a wonderful Thai dish. Dried basil and dried lime leaves don't retain enough fragrance or flavor, so I never use them, even if that's all I can find. In Thailand the fresh wild lime leaves are sliced crosswise into very thin strips and sprinkled over the top just before serving, so you may want to try it that way as well.

Thais often prepare this dish with enormous freshwater shrimp, with head and shell left on, or with lobster. *Choo chee* is also prepared with large chunks of freshwater fish, so try it with catfish fillets or pieces of trout, or with a meaty, white saltwater fish such as sea bass, snapper, or cod.

MOO PAHT PEHT
Pork Sautéed in Red Curry Paste

This spicy-hot stir-fry is a terrific traditional dish. Just be aware that its chili heat can set your mouth on fire. Enjoy it in small bites with lots of jasmine rice, accompanied by something sweet like Son-in-Law Eggs (page 36) and a bowl of soothing, Chinese-style soup with bean curd and spinach (page 43).

The dish goes together quickly and lends itself to countless variations. For example, chunks of catfish or catfish fillets are often used in place of the pork; they are added to the fiery sauce and cooked just until tender. The classic Thai version is *moo bah paht peht,* made with wild boar instead of pork and spiked with beautiful, fragrant clusters of fresh, young green peppercorns.

3 tablespoons vegetable oil
3 tablespoons Red Curry Paste (page 171)
1/2 pound pork, thinly sliced into strips about 1 1/2 inches long and 3/4 inch wide
2 tablespoons fish sauce
2 tablespoons water
2 teaspoons sugar
12 green beans, trimmed and cut into 2-inch lengths
1/2 cup diced eggplant (1-inch dice)
A handful of fresh graprao basil leaves, or other fresh basil leaves or fresh mint leaves
12 fresh wild lime leaves
9 long, thin sweet red pepper strips

In a wok or medium skillet, heat the oil over low heat until very warm but not hot. Add the curry paste, which should sizzle gently as soon as it meets the oil, and press and stir it into the oil. Cook the curry paste, mashing it into the oil, until it is well blended, fragrant, and shiny, about 3 minutes. Add the meat and stir-fry to brown it and coat it evenly with the curry paste, about 2 minutes.

Add the fish sauce, water, sugar, green beans, and eggplant; mix well. Cook for 2 to 3 minutes, stirring occasionally. Remove from the heat and stir in most of the basil leaves, lime leaves, and red pepper strips, reserving a little for garnish. Transfer to a serving plate, garnish with the reserved leaves and red pepper strips, and serve warm.

SERVES 4.

NOTE: Omit the wild lime leaves and fresh basil if they are difficult to find.

GAI PAHT BAI GRAPRAO
Chicken with Graprao Basil

Graprao basil is sometimes called holy basil, perhaps because in India it is associated with the god Vishnu and is grown on temple grounds. It has a unique, pungent flavor, both spicy and sharp. The leaves are dull rather than shiny, have a serrated edge, and wilt faster than other fresh herb leaves; they must be used as soon as possible once they are purchased. It is difficult to find this basil in the United States, so Thai restaurants usually substitute fresh mint leaves, but any kind of fresh basil will work well. This chili-hot dish over rice is one of my favorite Thai meals.

1 *chicken breast half*
1 *chicken thigh*
1 *tablespoon vegetable oil*
1 *tablespoon coarsely chopped garlic*
1 *tablespoon minced fresh* kii noo *chili or serrano chili*
2 *tablespoons fish sauce*
1 *tablespoon water*
1 *teaspoon dark soy sauce*
1 *tablespoon sugar*
1 *cup* graprao *basil leaves or other fresh basil leaves or fresh mint leaves*
3 *large fresh red* chee fah *chilies, sliced on the diagonal into thin ovals, or 9 long, thin sweet red pepper strips*

Bone and skin the chicken breast and thigh. You should have about 1/2 pound meat. Cut the meat into 1-inch chunks and then finely chop it with a cleaver, or slice it into thin, bite-sized pieces. Set aside.

Heat a wok or large, deep skillet over medium-high heat. Add the oil and swirl it to coat the surface. Drop a piece of the garlic into the pan. If it sizzles immediately, the oil is ready. Add the garlic and toss briefly. Add the minced chili and toss until the garlic begins to turn golden, about 15 seconds. Add the chicken and stir-fry until it changes color, about 1 minute.

Add the fish sauce, water, and soy sauce and stir-fry to combine well with the meat, about 1 minute. Add the sugar and stir-fry for another 30 seconds. Add the basil and sliced chilies and toss and stir-fry until the basil begins to wilt.

Transfer the chicken mixture to a serving bowl and serve hot.

SERVES 4.

NOTE: If you use a food processor to chop the meat you'll end up with a fine paste that doesn't stir-fry well. It's better to chop the meat by hand or to slice it into thin, bite-sized pieces. Thais often make this dish with ground pork instead of ground chicken. Ground turkey would work well, too.

GAI PAHT MEHT MAMUANG HIMAPAHN
Chicken Stir-Fried with Cashews

Cashews are popular in Thailand, either fried as a snack or cooked with dried red chilies and chicken in this Chinese-inspired dish.

2 tablespoons vegetable oil
15 small dried red chilies
3/4 pound chicken breast, boned, skinned, if desired, and thinly sliced crosswise
  into 1/2-inch-wide strips
1 small onion, peeled and sliced lengthwise into thick wedges
1 tablespoon fish sauce
1 teaspoon soy sauce
1/2 teaspoon sugar
1/2 cup dry-roasted, salted cashews

Heat a wok or medium skillet over medium heat. Add the oil and swirl to coat the surface. When the oil is hot but not smoking, add the chilies and stir-fry for 1 minute. They should darken but not blacken and burn. Remove the chilies with a slotted spoon and set aside.

Increase the heat to medium high, add the chicken, and stir-fry until it changes color and is cooked through, about 2 minutes. Add the onion and stir-fry until onion begins to wilt, about 1 minute. Add the fish sauce, soy sauce, and sugar and continue stir-frying for another minute. Add the cashews and the reserved chilies and stir well. Transfer to a serving platter and serve hot or warm.

SERVES 4.

NOTE: You can use raw cashews for this recipe. Begin by toasting them or frying them briefly in oil to bring out their flavor. You'll probably need a little extra fish sauce or salt as well.

This dish would also be good with shrimp instead of chicken.

MOO PAHT BRIOW WAHN
Pork with Vegetables in Sweet-Sour Sauce

Thai sweet-sour dishes have a fresh, clear flavor. This one is an excellent companion for a rich, spicy curry, and it also makes a good one-dish meal over rice.

2 tablespoons vegetable oil
1 tablespoon coarsely chopped garlic
1/4 pound pork tenderloin, thinly sliced across the grain
1 cup small cauliflower florets
2 tablespoons water
1 small onion, sliced lengthwise into thick wedges
3 tablespoons fish sauce
2 tablespoons sugar
1/4 teaspoon salt
1/2 small cucumber, peeled and sliced on the diagonal into thick ovals (1/2 cup)
6 to 8 cherry tomatoes, halved lengthwise

Heat a wok or large, deep skillet over medium-high heat. Add the oil and swirl to coat the surface. When the oil is very hot, drop a piece of the garlic into the pan. If it sizzles immediately, the oil is ready. Add the garlic and toss until it just begins to turn golden, about 15 seconds. Add the pork and stir-fry until it changes color, about 1 minute. Stir in the cauliflower florets and toss them until they are shiny with oil. Add the water and allow it to cook away without stirring. When the cauliflower is tender and the pan is almost dry, add the onion, fish sauce, sugar, and salt and toss to combine everything well.

Add the cucumber, tossing well. When all the ingredients are cooked but still crisp, stir in the tomatoes and toss once. Quickly remove from the heat and transfer to a serving plate. Serve hot.

SERVES 4.

NOTE: Chicken or shrimp can be substituted for the pork.

MOO PAHT KING
Pork Stir-Fried with Fresh Ginger

Market vendors in Thailand court customers with small mountains of beautifully shredded ginger alongside piles of tender, fresh cloud ear mushrooms and slabs of pork. Here you'll have to shred your own ginger and, if you opt to use them, soak the dried cloud ears, but once that's done the dish is almost ready.

2 tablespoons vegetable oil
1 tablespoon coarsely chopped garlic
1/4 pound thinly sliced pork
1/2 cup long, thin peeled fresh ginger strips
1 small onion, sliced lengthwise into thick wedges
1 tablespoon fish sauce
1 cup fresh small oyster mushrooms or any fresh mushroom, thinly sliced lengthwise
1 tablespoon soy sauce
3 fresh red chee fah chilies or 9 long, thin sweet red pepper strips
1 tablespoon water
1 teaspoon sugar

Heat a wok or a large, deep skillet over medium-high heat until hot. Add the oil and swirl to coat the surface. When the oil is very hot, drop a piece of the garlic into the pan. If it sizzles immediately, the oil is ready. Add the garlic and toss until it just begins to turn golden, about 15 seconds. Add the pork and stir-fry until it is no longer pink, about 2 minutes.

Add the ginger and toss to coat with the oil. Let it cook about 1 minute and then add the onion and fish sauce and toss to mix them in. Add the mushrooms and soy sauce and stir-fry until mushrooms have softened and are shiny, about 1 minute. Add the chilies, water, and sugar and toss well. Cook without stirring for 1 minute. Taste the sauce to see that it has a pleasing balance of salty and sweet and adjust as needed. Transfer to a serving platter and serve hot.

SERVES 4.

NOTE: Chicken or shrimp may be substituted for the pork.
Dried cloud ears may be substituted for the fresh mushrooms. Soak about 1 tablespoon tiny dried cloud ears in warm water to cover until softened, about 30 minutes. Drain and place on a cutting board. Check them over with your fingers, cutting off and discarding any hard little navels you may find. Slice the cloud ears into long, thin shreds and proceed as directed.

KAI JIOW
Plain Omelet

Here is the easiest of egg dishes. It is always served with a small saucer of Sri Racha sauce, a volcanic chili-garlic purée that can be found in bottles in Thai and Southeast Asian markets.

4 eggs
1 tablespoon fish sauce
1 teaspoon water
2 tablespoons vegetable oil
Sri Racha sauce or other hot chili sauce

In a bowl, whisk together the eggs, fish sauce, and water until well blended. In a wok or medium skillet, heat the oil over medium heat until very hot. Add a drop of the egg mixture to the oil. If it sizzles and blooms immediately, the oil is ready.

Pour in the eggs and tilt the pan to spread them evenly. The eggs will begin to puff in all directions. Using a spatula, pull the puffy edges in toward the center, working around the omelet to allow all of the liquid pooled in the center to run out and extend the borders of the omelet. After about 2 minutes, when the edges are golden and the top is opaque and is almost set, gently flip the omelet over and brown the other side for 1 minute.

Turn the omelet out onto a plate and serve with small saucers of Sri Racha sauce.

SERVES 4 TO 6.

NOTE: Thais make this dish with lots of oil, which produces a puffy, golden brown omelet. If you'd like to try to make it that way, increase the oil to about 1/4 cup.

To make Omelet with Minced Pork *(kai jiow moo sahp),* stir 1/4 pound ground pork into the beaten eggs, breaking it up a bit. Cook the omelet in the same manner as the plain one, but a little longer. I also like to mix in sliced green onions and chopped fresh cilantro leaves, although they are nontraditional additions.

KAI YAHT SAI
Omelet Stuffed with Minced Pork

These omelets are plump packets of savory minced pork sautéed with tomatoes, onions, and green beans.

FILLING
2 tablespoons vegetable oil
1 tablespoon finely chopped garlic
1/4 cup coarsely chopped onion
1/2 pound ground pork
1/4 cup thinly sliced green beans (sliced crosswise)
2 tablespoons fish sauce
1/3 cup coarsely chopped cherry tomatoes or plum tomatoes
2 teaspoons sugar
1/4 teaspoon freshly ground pepper
A handful of coarsely chopped fresh cilantro leaves

OMELETS
6 eggs
1 tablespoon fish sauce
1 teaspoon water
About 3 tablespoons vegetable oil

A handful of fresh cilantro sprigs
Sri Racha sauce or other hot chili sauce

To make the filling, heat a wok or medium skillet over medium-high heat. Add the oil and swirl to coat the surface. When the oil is very hot, drop a piece of the garlic into the pan. If the garlic sizzles immediately, the oil is ready. Add the garlic and toss until it just begins to turn golden, about 5 seconds. Reduce the heat to medium and add the onion. Stir-fry until it begins to wilt, about 1 minute. Add the pork and stir-fry until it is no longer pink, about 2 minutes.

Add the green beans and fish sauce and toss to combine. Add the tomatoes and sugar and toss again. Simmer until the sauce thickens slightly, about 3 minutes. Mix in the pepper and cilantro and transfer to a small bowl. Set aside.

To make the omelets, in a medium bowl, whisk together the eggs, fish sauce, and water. Heat 1 tablespoon of the oil in a wok or heavy 12-inch skillet over medium heat until very hot. Add about one third of the beaten egg, and tilt the pan to spread the egg into a thin even sheet. Using a spatula, lift up the edges of the egg sheet and push them in a bit with your spatula, allowing the liquid pooled in the center to run underneath and cook as well. Cook until the egg is opaque and the top is almost set, about 1 minute. Increase the heat a little and cook until the bottom of the omelet is golden brown, loosening the edges with your spatula and shaking the pan to slide the omelet back and forth, about 1 minute longer.

Gently flip the omelet over and cook the other side just until set, about 15 seconds. Remove from the heat and gently flip the omelet onto a platter, golden side down. Spoon about one third of the pork filling in a line down the center of the omelet. Fold in opposite sides, first the top and then the bottom, then the right and the left, and turn the package over, seam side down. Set aside on a serving platter while you cook and fill the remaining omelets in the same way, adding oil to the pan as needed.

Garnish the platter with cilantro and a small saucer of Sri Racha sauce and serve hot or warm.

SERVES 6.

NOTE: You can make the filling a day ahead and chill it; reheat it gently when you're ready to cook the omelet.

If this business of folding the egg into packets drives you crazy, simply place a stripe of filling down the center of each omelet and fold it in half.

KAI TOON
Steamed Eggs with Green Onions and Fried Garlic in Oil

Kai toon is comfort food in any language. A perfect balance for spicy dishes, this silky custard goes beautifully with a crisp vegetable stir-fry and a plate of rice. Since it's simple to prepare and easy to love, I use it to stretch my menu when extra guests arrive. If you'd like to make it more substantial, add a little chopped pork or shrimp or some cooked crab meat to the eggs before steaming.

2 eggs
3/4 cup water
1 tablespoon fish sauce
1/2 teaspoon freshly ground white pepper
1 tablespoon thinly sliced green onion (green tops only)
2 tablespoons Fried Garlic in Oil (page 184)

Fill a wok or a steamer pan with water and bring to a rolling boil over high heat. Meanwhile, combine the eggs, water, fish sauce, pepper, and green onion in a small, heatproof mixing bowl. Beat with a fork until everything is well blended.

When you have a strong, steady flow of steam, carefully place the bowl of eggs on a steamer rack above the water; cover the bowl with a paper towel to prevent condensed steam from dripping in. Place a lid on the wok or steamer and reduce the heat to maintain a steady flow of steam. Steam the eggs until they are firm, pale yellow, and slightly puffed up, 10 to 15 minutes.

When the eggs are done, remove the cover, taking care to keep any steam that has condensed inside the cover from dripping into the custard. Remove the bowl from the steamer rack and pour the garlic and oil over the top of the eggs. Serve hot, warm, or at room temperature.

SERVES 4 TO 6.

KAI LEUK KOEY
Son-in-Law Eggs

This delicious dish reminds me of weddings in Thailand, which, like all Thai celebrations, involve lots of company and wonderful food. The bride's family treats dozens and sometimes even hundreds of guests to an elaborate banquet. The feast is the result of days of cooking by local caterers, usually working out of a field kitchen in the host's backyard. For traditional *kai leuk koey*, hard-cooked duck eggs are fried until golden and drenched with a piquant, sweet-sharp tamarind sauce. Each guest scoops an egg from the pool of sauce and enjoys it over rice. I like to serve these eggs as finger food, halved or quartered lengthwise and wrapped in a leaf of Boston lettuce.

TAMARIND SAUCE
1/3 cup Tamarind Liquid (page 185)
1/4 cup palm sugar or brown sugar
3 tablespoons fish sauce
3 tablespoons water

EGGS
Vegetable oil for deep-frying
6 shallots, thinly sliced crosswise and separated into rings
6 garlic cloves, thinly sliced lengthwise
6 eggs, hard-cooked and shelled
Coarsely ground dried red chilies

To make the sauce, combine the tamarind, sugar, fish sauce, and water in a small, heavy saucepan. Bring to a boil over medium heat, stirring to dissolve the sugar. Reduce the heat and simmer for 10 minutes, stirring occasionally. Remove from the heat and transfer to a small serving bowl. Set aside until serving time.

To make the eggs, pour the oil into a wok or deep, heavy skillet to a depth of 3 inches. Heat the oil over medium heat to 350° to 375°F. Drop a piece of the shallot into the pan. If it sizzles immediately, the oil is ready. Add the shallots and cook until brown but not burned, 1 to 2 minutes. Remove with a slotted spoon and drain on paper towels. Add the garlic and cook until golden brown, about 1 minute. Remove with a slotted spoon and drain on paper towels.

If the eggs are wet, pat them dry with a paper towel. Line a medium bowl with paper towels. Gently slide 3 of the eggs, one by one, down the side of the wok into the hot oil. Use your spatula or a slotted spoon to keep them from resting on the bottom of the wok. Cook on all sides until golden brown and crisp, turning occasionally and keeping them floating, about 7 minutes. Remove with a slotted spoon and set aside in the paper-lined bowl. Repeat with the remaining eggs.

To serve, halve the eggs lengthwise and arrange them, yolk side up, on a platter. Sprinkle with some of the fried shallot and garlic and ground chilies. Place the bowl of sauce in the center of the platter and sprinkle with the garlic and the shallots. Serve warm or at room temperature.

SERVES 6 TO 8.

NOTE: You can prepare the sauce several hours ahead and let it stand, covered, at room temperature. Reheat gently over low heat just before serving time.

PAHK BOONG FAI DAENG
Water Spinach in Flames

Pahk boong is the Thai name for a deep green vegetable with hollow stems and arrowhead-shaped leaves. It is called *ong choy* in Cantonese, and is so popular with Asians that it is sold fresh in markets in cities in North America with large Asian populations.

The dish acquired its picturesque name from the manner in which it is prepared by skillful restaurant chefs. When the vegetable is tossed into the smoking hot oil, a tower of flames shoots into the air. Being wary of columns of flame in my kitchen, I don't seek to achieve this effect, but if you do find your *pahk boong* on fire, the blaze is quickly over, and it does add a very nice charred flavor to the dish.

1 bunch water spinach, or 2 bunches regular spinach (about 2 pounds)
2 tablespoons fish sauce
1 tablespoon brown bean sauce (dao jiow)
1 tablespoon sugar
1/4 cup vegetable oil
2 tablespoons coarsely chopped garlic
1/2 teaspoon freshly ground pepper

Trim away and discard the bottom 2 inches of coarse, woody ends of the water spinach. Cut the remaining stems into 2-inch lengths and place them in a bowl. Cut the leafier top portions into 2-inch lengths as well, and put them in another bowl. You'll have about 8 cups total; set aside. If you are using regular spinach, trim away and discard the stems. Combine fish sauce, bean sauce, and sugar in a small bowl; set alongside the stove.

Heat a wok or large, deep skillet over high heat. Add the oil and swirl to coat the surface. When the oil is smoking hot, add the garlic, toss continuously for 10 seconds, and add the spinach stems. Toss and turn them quickly, then let them sizzle undisturbed for 1 minute.

Add the fish sauce mixture, toss to mix with the oil, and add the leafy portions of the water spinach or all of the regular spinach. Toss and turn the spinach quickly until it begins to wilt, then transfer it to a serving platter, along with any cooking liquid from the pan. Serve hot or warm.

SERVES 4 TO 6.

NOTE: This recipe works well with any of the sturdy, leafy Asian vegetables available in North American markets, including bok choy, yu choy, and baby bok choy, as well as broccoli rabe. Adjust the cooking time according to the tenderness of the vegetable you choose.

TOME YUM GOONG
Spicy Shrimp Soup with Lemongrass and Lime

> *Tome yum goong* is the perfect centerpiece for a Thai meal, and for all its glory it's actually quite simple to make. Roasted chili paste, *nahm prik pao,* is the secret weapon that makes this soup diabolically good—and exceedingly hot. Thais use lemongrass as a healing herb, with particular power over colds, so this clear, sharp soup could be just what the doctor ordered if you're caring for a patient who loves chili. Serve it with a good-sized mound of rice.

4 cups Basic Chicken Stock (page 186) or other light chicken stock
3 large stalks fresh lemongrass
12 fresh wild lime leaves
6 fresh kii noo *chilies*
Juice of 1 lime, (about 2 1/2 tablespoons)
3 slender green onions, cut into 1-inch lengths
1 tablespoon Roasted Chili Paste (page 153)
1 cup well-drained, whole canned straw mushrooms
1/2 pound shrimp, peeled, with tails left on, and deveined
2 tablespoons fish sauce

In a large saucepan bring the stock to a boil over medium heat. Meanwhile, trim the lemongrass stalks. Cut away and discard the grassy tops of the stalks, leaving stalks about 6 inches long. Cut away any hard root section to leave a clean, smooth, flat base at the root end below the bulb. Remove and discard tough outer leaves. Using the blunt edge of a cleaver blade or heavy knife, bruise each stalk, whacking it firmly at 2-inch intervals and rolling it over to bruise the stalk on all sides.

Add the bruised lemongrass stalks and 6 of the lime leaves to the boiling stock and reduce the heat to a simmer. Cook until the stock is fragrant and the lemongrass has changed from a fresh green to a dull khaki green, about 5 minutes.

Meanwhile, stem the chilies and place them under the flat side of a cleaver or a chef's knife. Crush them gently until they begin to split. Place the crushed chilies in a large serving bowl and add the lime juice, green onions, and the remaining 6 lime leaves. Set aside.

Remove and discard the lemongrass. Increase the heat to high and add the chili paste and mushrooms. When the soup has boiled for 1 minute, add the fish sauce and shrimp and cook until the shrimp are pink, opaque, and firm, no more than 1 minute.

Remove the soup from the heat and quickly pour it into the

serving bowl over the chili mixture. Stir quickly to combine, and taste for seasoning. It should be intensely sour, salty, and hot. Adjust with lime juice, fish sauce, and chili paste as needed.

Serve at once.

SERVES 6.

NOTE: You need fresh lemongrass for this soup, but you can omit the wild lime leaves if they're difficult to find. Three fresh serrano chilies, halved lengthwise, can replace the crushed *kii noo* chilies. If you want to tone down the heat, omit the crushed chilies or serve them on the side.

TOME KHA GAI
Chicken-Coconut Soup with Galanga

This extraordinary soup is rich with coconut milk and sharp with the magical flavors of galanga, lemongrass, and wild lime leaves. *Kha* is galanga, a member of the ginger family with a strong citrus flavor and scent. Unlike lemongrass, it retains much of its unique flavor when dried, so you can make a delicious *tome kha gai* even if you can't find fresh Asian herbs. Galanga is also available frozen in many Southeast Asian markets in the West. This dish calls for something spicy hot and something salty, so serve it with Shrimp Stir-Fried with Roasted Chili Paste (page 153) and Spinach with Black Pepper and Garlic (page 38).

1 whole chicken breast
2 chicken thighs
4 stalks fresh lemongrass
4 1/2 cups coconut milk
1 1/2 cups Basic Chicken Stock (page 186) or other light chicken stock
20 quarter-sized slices fresh galanga
10 whole black peppercorns
12 fresh wild lime leaves
1 cup well-drained, whole canned straw mushrooms, halved lengthwise
2 tablespoons fish sauce
2 tablespoons freshly squeezed lime juice

Bone and skin the chicken breast and thighs. You should have about 1 pound meat. Cut the meat into large bite-sized pieces; set aside.

Cut away and discard the grassy tops of the lemongrass stalks, leaving stalks about 6 inches long. Cut away any hard root section to leave a clean, smooth, flat base at the root end below the bulb. Remove and discard tough outer leaves. Using the blunt edge of a Chinese cleaver or heavy knife, bruise each stalk, whacking it firmly at 2-inch intervals and rolling it over to bruise the stalk on all sides. Cut each stalk crosswise into 4 pieces; set aside.

In a 3-quart saucepan, combine the coconut milk and chicken stock and bring to a gentle boil over medium-high heat. Stir in the lemongrass, chicken, galanga, peppercorns, and 6 of the lime leaves. Reduce the heat to maintain a simmer and cook until the chicken is done, 10 to15 minutes.

When the chicken is cooked, add the mushrooms and remove from the heat. Stir in the fish sauce and lime juice. Taste and add more fish sauce and lime juice if you like. Transfer to a serving bowl and serve hot.

SERVES 6 TO 8.

NOTE: Thai cooks usually leave the seasoning herbs in the soup, even though they aren't eaten. If you like, you can strain the soup to remove the lemongrass, galanga, peppercorns, and lime leaves, and then return the soup and chicken to the pan.

Fresh straw mushrooms are readily available in Thailand but are seldom seen in the West. You can use a handful of small fresh button mushrooms instead, halving them lengthwise and allowing an extra 1 or 2 minutes for them to cook.

Even if you can't find all the fresh herbs this recipe calls for, you can still make a delicious *tome kha gai*. For lemongrass and wild lime leaves, simply add a little extra lime juice. For fresh galanga, substitute the same amount of frozen galanga or a handful of dried galanga slices. You could even use an equal amount of fresh ginger slices instead.

GAENG JEUTE DAO HOO
Clear Soup with Spinach and Bean Curd

> *Gaeng* is "soup" or "stew," and *jeute* means "mild-flavored." This soup is the type that Thai cooks serve as a soothing foil to the sting of chilies and the sweet-sharp notes of palm sugar, tamarind, and lime. Traditionally, soup was served as a beverage with meals. While that custom is changing, soup is still eaten along with rice and other dishes rather than as a separate course.

4 cups Basic Chicken Stock (page 186) or other light chicken stock
2 cups bite-sized chunks fresh bean curd
1 tablespoon fish sauce
1/4 teaspoon freshly ground white pepper
3 small green onions, thinly sliced crosswise
A handful of small spinach leaves, stemmed and left whole, or large leaves torn
  into bite-sized pieces

In a medium saucepan, bring the stock to a gentle boil over medium heat. Add the bean curd, fish sauce, and pepper and simmer for 1 to 2 minutes.

Taste and adjust seasoning with more fish sauce and pepper. Gently stir in the green onions and spinach, remove from the heat, and serve.

SERVES 6.

GAENG JEUTE WOON SEN
Clear Soup with Minced Pork and Bean Thread Noodles

Bean thread noodles, *or woon sen,* are delicate, clear noodles made from mung beans. They are also called glass noodles, cellophane noodles, or silver noodles, because they are silvery when dry and clear once they are cooked. Bean threads cook quickly, so they are dropped into soups at the last minute to absorb flavors and add a pleasing texture. Because the noodles and pork make this *gaeng jeute* more substantial than *gaeng jeute dao hoo,* I use it as an easy main course along with an omelet, a vegetable stir-fry, and jasmine rice.

4 cups Basic Chicken Stock (page 186) or other light chicken stock
1/4 pound coarsely ground pork
1 tablespoon finely minced garlic
1/2 teaspoon freshly ground white pepper, plus white pepper for serving
1/2 teaspoon salt
1 packet (2-ounces) bean thread noodles
1 tablespoon fish sauce
3 slender green onions, thinly sliced crosswise
2 tablespoons Fried Garlic in Oil (page 184)
A small handful of fresh cilantro leaves

In a medium saucepan, bring the stock to a rolling boil over medium heat. Meanwhile, in a small bowl, combine pork, garlic, pepper, and salt and set aside. Place the bean thread noodles in a bowl, cover with warm water, and soak until softened, about 30 minutes.

Drop small clumps of the seasoned pork into the boiling stock. Skim off and discard any foam that rises to the surface as the meat cooks. Simmer for 3 minutes. Drain the noodles and dump the tangle onto your cutting board. Cut through the pile of noodles crosswise and lengthwise. Add the noodles to the boiling soup. Stir in the fish sauce and green onions and remove from the heat. Transfer to a serving bowl and add a sprinkling of pepper, the garlic and oil, and the cilantro leaves. Serve hot.

SERVES 6.

NOTE: Strips of cloud ear mushrooms are often added to this Chinese-style soup. Soak a small handful in warm water to cover for 30 minutes. Drain and trim away any hard little navels, then slice the cloud ears into long, thin strips. Add to the soup with the bean thread noodles. You could also use large, dried Chinese black mushrooms, which have been soaked in the same way, stemmed, and cut into strips, or slices of any fresh mushroom.

KAO MUN GAI
Hainan Chicken and Rice with Ginger Brown Bean Sauce

Kao mun gai originated on Hainan Island, off the southern coast of China in the Gulf of Tonkin. Most large Thai towns support a restaurant specializing in this dish, and it is popular throughout Southeast Asia. Chicken is served in chunks over rice that has been cooked in the rich, oily stock left over from cooking the chicken. This explains the Thai name, which literally means "rice cooked in chicken fat." The chicken and rice come with crisp cucumber slices, a small bowl of clear chicken stock with green onions, and a distinctive, pungent dipping sauce made with garlic, ginger, dark soy sauce, and vinegar.

1 whole chicken (about 4 pounds)
5 sprigs fresh cilantro, preferably with roots intact
1 teaspoon salt

GINGER BROWN BEAN SAUCE
1/4 cup brown bean sauce (dao jiow)
2 tablespoons white vinegar
1 tablespoon dark soy sauce
2 teaspoons sugar
1 tablespoon finely minced fresh ginger
2 teaspoons finely minced garlic
1 teaspoon finely minced fresh kii noo chili or serrano chili

1 tablespoon coarsely chopped garlic
3 cups jasmine rice or other long-grain white rice
3 tablespoons thinly sliced green onion (sliced crosswise)
2 or 3 small cucumbers, peeled and sliced crosswise into 1/4-inch-thick rounds

Select a 3-quart saucepan with a tight-fitting lid and place the chicken in it. Add the cilantro, salt, and enough water to cover the chicken by about 1 inch. Bring to a boil, uncovered, over medium heat. Reduce the heat to maintain an active simmer and cook, occasionally skimming off and discarding any foam that rises to the surface, until tender, about 40 minutes.

While the chicken simmers, combine all of the ingredients for the sauce in a small bowl and mix well. Set aside.

When the chicken is done, remove the pan from the heat. Lift out the chicken and place it on a platter; set aside. Measure out 3 cups of the chicken stock; pour off the remaining stock into a small saucepan and reserve it to serve with the rice. In the same saucepan in which the chicken was cooked, combine the 3 cups chicken stock, garlic, and rice. Stirring occasionally, bring to an active boil over medium heat. When the chicken stock boils away to expose the surface of the rice, stir once more, cover tightly, and reduce the heat to very low. Cook over low heat for an additional 25 minutes without uncovering. Remove from the heat, still covered, and let stand undisturbed for 15 minutes. Remove the lid, stir to separate and fluff rice grains, and set aside. Bone chicken and cut meat into large chunks, about 2 inches by 1 inch.

To serve, reheat the reserved chicken stock. Remove from the heat and sprinkle with the green onions. Scoop a serving of rice onto individual plates. Top each mound of rice with chunks of chicken and slices of cucumber. Serve warm or at room temperature, with a bowl of the chicken stock and a bowl of the bean sauce on the side.

SERVES 6.

KAO PAHT MOO
Fried Rice with Pork

Fried rice is a fast, one-dish meal. Cold rice works best for frying, since it breaks up easily into individual grains, so plan on cooking enough rice to ensure leftovers to refrigerate for making this dish. If you want country-style fried rice, fry an egg per person in hot oil and place on top of each serving of rice.

1 lime, cut lengthwise into 6 wedges
2 small cucumbers, peeled and sliced on the diagonal into thick ovals
1/3 cup fish sauce
Sliced fresh hot chilies
4 to 5 cups cold, cooked Jasmine Rice (page 164), preferably chilled
2 tablespoons vegetable oil
1 tablespoon coarsely chopped garlic
3/4 cup coarsely chopped yellow onion
1/4 pound pork, thinly sliced
1 large egg, lightly beaten
2 tablespoons fish sauce
1/2 teaspoon sugar

Prepare the lime and cucumbers and arrange on a serving platter. Pour the fish sauce into a small bowl and add the chilies; set the bowl near the edge of the platter.

Prepare the rice by crumbling it with your fingers, breaking up all the lumps into individual grains; set aside.

Heat a wok or a large, deep skillet over high heat. Add the oil and swirl to coat the surface. When the oil is very hot, drop a piece of the garlic into the pan. If it sizzles immediately, the oil is ready. Add the garlic and toss until it just begins to turn golden, about 15 seconds. Add the onion and toss until it begins to wilt and become translucent, about 1 minute.

Add the pork and stir-fry until it is no longer pink, about 2 minutes. Add the egg and tilt the pan to spread it into a thin sheet. As soon as the egg begins to set, scramble it to break it into small lumps. Add the rice and toss to coat it with the oil. Add the fish sauce and sugar and stir-fry to distribute ingredients well.

When the rice is hot throughout and all the ingredients are mixed well, transfer to the already garnished serving platter. Guests can add lime juice and fish sauce with chilies to taste. Serve hot or warm.

SERVES 4.

NOTE: This recipe is also good made with chicken, ham, or shrimp instead of pork.

KAO TOME
Rice Porridge with Minced Pork, Fried Garlic, and Green Onions

Thais always cook more rice than they think they'll need, in case guests come by or the family is especially hungry. Leftovers are soon turned into fried rice or this homey soup. *Kao tome* means "boiled rice," and it's comfort food, perfect for breakfast, a late-night supper, or as a mild, filling meal when you're feeling sick. Thais consider it the perfect treatment for a hangover.

4 cups Basic Chicken Stock (page 186) or other light chicken stock
Chili-Vinegar Sauce (page 188)
2 cups cooked white rice
1/4 pound minced pork or coarsely chopped chicken meat
1 tablespoon fish sauce, plus fish sauce for serving
1 teaspoon freshly ground pepper
1/2 cup Fried Garlic in Oil (page 184)
3 tablespoons thinly sliced green onion (sliced crosswise)
A handful of fresh cilantro leaves

In a saucepan over medium heat, bring the stock to a gentle boil. Meanwhile, prepare the Chili-Vinegar Sauce and set aside. Stir the rice into the boiling stock. When the stock returns to a boil, add the pork, pinching off small amounts and dropping them in one by one. Cook until the pork is done, about 5 minutes. Stir in the 1 tablespoon fish sauce and pepper.

Remove from the heat and ladle into individual serving bowls. Top each serving with a spoonful of garlic and oil, green onion, and cilantro leaves. Serve with the Chili-Vinegar Sauce and additional fish sauce.

SERVES 6.

NOTE: *Kao tome* often comes with an egg coddled in the simmering broth. You could add a poached egg to each serving bowl if you like.

Other traditional accompaniments you may want to offer include ground dried red chilies, minced fresh ginger, salty Chinese pickled cabbage such as Tientsin pickled vegetable, and bits of the sweet, dark, pickled giant radish called *chai po.*

YUM GOONG HAENG
Dried Shrimp with Shallots, Chilies, and Lime

I discovered this recipe in *Adventures in Thai Food and Culture,* by Ms. Krissnee Ruangkritya, who owns the Siam Restaurant in Orlando, Florida. Her pungent dried shrimp relish took only minutes to make, and when I tried it with rice I felt as though I were back in up-country Thailand, eating supper with my students. The relish epitomizes the four intense flavors of Thai food: the saltiness of dried shrimp and fish sauce, the punch of fiery chilies, the soothing sweetness of sugar, and the clear, sour bite of lime. It is terrific as a condiment with *kao tome* (page 48), the Thai version of Chinese rice porridge that is so popular for breakfast or midnight snacks. It is also good with a mound of steaming jasmine rice.

1/2 cup dried shrimp
1/4 cup freshly squeezed lime juice
2 tablespoons fish sauce
2 tablespoons sugar
2 tablespoons thinly sliced shallot (sliced crosswise)
2 teaspoons thinly sliced fresh kii noo *chili or serrano chili (sliced crosswise)*

Soak the dried shrimp in warm water to cover for 5 minutes; drain. Pound the shrimp lightly in a mortar with a pestle, or coarsely chop them, until they begin to break down.

Combine the shrimp with all the remaining ingredients in a small bowl and stir well.

SERVES 4 TO 6.

YUM KAI KEM
Salty Egg Salad

> *Yum kai kem* is a simple, country-style accompaniment to rice. It's often paired with green curries as a sharp, salty complement to their rich, fiery heat.

3 Salty Eggs (page 182), cooked and cooled to room temperature
6 fresh kii noo chilies or 2 serrano chilies, thinly sliced crosswise
2 tablespoons coarsely chopped shallot
2 tablespoons freshly squeezed lime juice

Peel the eggs, halve them lengthwise, and arrange them on a small serving dish. Sprinkle the chili slices and shallots over the eggs. Drizzle with the lime juice and serve.

SERVES 6.

PAHT THAI
Rice Noodles Stir-Fried Thai Style

Paht Thai is a noodle dish almost everyone seems to like. A tangle of slender rice noodles is sautéed with garlic, shallots, and an orchestra of sweet, sour, and salty ingredients that play a piquant symphony of Thai flavors. A handful of fresh bean sprouts provides a cooling contrast to the hot, seasoned noodles, and circles of lime invite you to bring sourness to center stage as you begin to eat.

Traditional ingredients are salty dried shrimp; crispy pieces of fried, pressed bean curd; sweet-sour nuggets of pickled white radish; chopped peanuts; flat, green garlic chives; and a balanced chorus—sweet, sour, salty, hot—of palm sugar, tamarind, vinegar, lime, brown bean sauce, and crushed dried red chilies. In Thailand an exotic palate cleanser often accompanies the prosaic bean sprouts: a beautiful wedge of purple-yellow banana flower.

Thai cooks blithely tinker with the classic formula to create signature versions, and you can, too. Siriluk Williams, owner of Sukothai Restaurant in Ft. Lauderdale, Florida, gave me her recipe for home-style *paht Thai.* I love its accessible ingredients, simple steps, and delicious results.

1/4 pound dried rice stick noodles
2 tablespoons vegetable oil
1 tablespoon coarsely chopped garlic
8 shrimp, peeled and deveined
1 egg, lightly beaten
1 tablespoon fish sauce
2 teaspoons sugar
2 tablespoons coarsely chopped, dry-roasted peanuts
1 cup bean sprouts
4 slender green onions, sliced in 1-inch lengths
1 lime, quartered lengthwise

Soak rice noodles in warm water to cover for 15 to 20 minutes. Meanwhile, prepare all the remaining ingredients and place them next to the stove, along with a small serving platter. When the noodles are very limp and white, drain and measure out 2 1/2 cups. Set these by the stove as well.

Heat a wok or large, deep skillet over medium-high heat. Add 1 tablespoon of the oil and swirl to coat the surface. When the oil is very hot, drop a piece of the garlic into the pan. If it sizzles immediately, the oil is ready. Add the garlic and toss until golden, about 30 seconds. Add the shrimp and toss until they turn pink and are opaque, no more than 1 minute. Remove from the pan and set aside.

Add the egg to the pan and tilt the pan to spread it into a thin sheet. As soon as it begins to set and is opaque, scramble it to break it into small lumps. Remove from the pan and set aside with the shrimp.

Add the remaining 1 tablespoon oil, heat for 30 seconds, and add the softened noodles. Using a spatula, spread and pull the noodles into a thin layer covering the surface of the pan. Then scrape them into a clump again and gently turn them over. Hook loops of noodles with the edge of the spatula and pull them up the sides, spreading them out into a layer again. Repeat this process several times as the stiff, white noodles soften and curl into ivory ringlets. Add the fish sauce and turn the noodles so they are evenly seasoned. Add the sugar and peanuts, turning the noodles a few more times.

Reserving a small handful for garnish, add the bean sprouts, along with the green onions and shrimp-egg mixture. Cook for 1 minute, turning often. Transfer the noodles to the serving platter and squeeze the juice of 2 lime wedges over the top. Garnish with remaining bean sprouts and lime wedges and serve at once.

SERVES 1 AS A MAIN COURSE, 2 AS AN APPETIZER.

NOTE: *Paht Thai* is traditionally made with a dried rice noodle that's flat and thin, similar to linguine. It's called *kwaytiow sen jahn,* sometimes translated on the package as chantaboon rice sticks. But any size and shape of dried rice noodle will work. Sealed airtight, unused dried noodles will keep for several months.

KWAYTIOW LAHT NAH
Rice Noodles with Beef and Chinese Broccoli in Cantonese-Style Gravy

> Thais serve this delicious salty-sour meat sauce over wide strips of soft rice noodles, but you could use any cooked noodles.

Chili-Vinegar Sauce (page 188)
3 tablespoons vegetable oil
1 pound soft, fresh rice noodle sheets, cut lengthwise into strips about 1 inch wide, or about 4 cups cooked noodles of any kind
2 tablespoons coarsely chopped garlic
1/2 pound beef, thinly sliced across the grain into strips 2 inches by 1 inch
3 cups cut-up Chinese broccoli (2-inch lengths) or small broccoli florets
1 tablespoon fish sauce
1 teaspoon dark soy sauce
1 tablespoon white vinegar
1 tablespoon brown bean sauce (dao jiow)
1 tablespoon sugar
1 tablespoon cornstarch, dissolved in 3 tablespoons cold water
1 cup chicken stock

Prepare the Chili-Vinegar Sauce and set aside. Heat a wok or large, deep skillet over medium heat. Add 2 tablespoons of the oil and swirl to coat the surface. Heat the oil until hot and add the noodles. Stir-fry gently for about 1 minute to separate them. Transfer to a large serving platter.

Add the remaining 1 tablespoon oil to the wok and heat until very hot. Add the garlic and toss until golden, about 30 seconds. Add the beef and stir-fry until it changes color, about 1 minute. Add the Chinese broccoli and stir-fry until it is bright green and shiny, about 30 seconds.

Add the fish sauce, soy sauce, vinegar, bean sauce, and sugar and toss well. Add the cornstarch mixture and stock, toss, and simmer until sauce thickens, 2 to 3 minutes. Pour the sauce over the noodles, toss, and serve at once with the Chili-Vinegar Sauce.

SERVES 4.

NOTE: An equal amount of chicken or pork may be substituted for the beef. To use peeled, deveined shrimp, cook them with the noodles and then pour the sauce over them both. For a vegetarian version, use a combination of fresh mushrooms and softened dried Chinese black mushrooms, thinly sliced into strips.

KWAYTIOW PAHT SI-YU
Rice Noodles with Soy Sauce, Chinese Broccoli, and Beef

A standard, one-dish lunch throughout Thailand, this is a fairly dry, stir-fried noodle similar to *paht Thai*. Instead of the sweet-sour-salty flavors of that dish, this one has a distinctly Chinese tone, with a dark, sweet richness and a milder taste that Thais sharpen with the usual noodle condiments—a chili and vinegar sauce, sugar, and crushed dried red chilies.

2 tablespoons dark sweet soy sauce or 2 tablespoons dark soy sauce and 1
  tablespoon molasses or sugar
1 tablespoon fish sauce
1/2 teaspoon freshly ground black pepper
3 to 4 tablespoons vegetable oil
1 tablespoon coarsely chopped garlic
4 cups Chinese broccoli, cut into 2-inch by 1-inch strips, or 3 cups small broccoli
  florets
1/2 pound flank steak, thinly sliced across the grain in strips 2 inches by 1 inch
1 pound soft, fresh flat rice noodle sheets, cut lengthwise into strips 1 inch wide
2 eggs, lightly beaten

CONDIMENTS
Chili-Vinegar Sauce (page 188)
Sugar
Coarsely ground dried red chili

Combine the soy sauce, fish sauce, and pepper in a small bowl and place next to the stove with all the other ingredients. Prepare the Chili-Vinegar Sauce and the other condiments and set them out on the table.

Heat a wok or large, deep skillet over medium-high heat. Add 2 tablespoons of the oil and swirl to coat the surface. When the oil is very hot, drop a piece of the garlic into the pan. If it sizzles immediately, the oil is ready. Add the garlic and toss until it begins to turn golden, about 15 seconds. Add the Chinese broccoli and stir-fry until tender, bright green, and shiny, about 2 minutes. Remove from the pan to a platter.

Add a little more oil to the wok, swirl to coat, and heat for 15 seconds. Add the beef and stir-fry until it's no longer pink, about 2 minutes. Remove from the pan to the platter with the bok choy.

Add about 1 tablespoon of oil to the wok and heat for 15 seconds. Add the noodles and toss until separated and heated through. Push the noodles to one side of the wok. Put 2 teaspoons of oil into the center of the wok and add the eggs. Cook without stirring for about 30 seconds. Scoop and toss everything gently, scrambling the eggs and mixing the ingredients together.

Add the soy sauce mixture and the reserved beef and Chinese broccoli and stir-fry until the noodles, meat, and vegetables are lightly coated with sauce, about 1 minute. Transfer to a heated platter and serve at once with small bowls of Chili-Vinegar Sauce, sugar, and chilies alongside.

SERVES 4.

NOTE: This dish works best with paper-thin beef slices. To make the beef easier to slice, first freeze it until stiff but not frozen solid, about 30 minutes. Then slice it across the grain as thinly as possible.

You can use any meat or seafood in place of beef, or firm bean curd if you prefer, adjusting the cooking time accordingly.

In Thailand this dish is made with Chinese broccoli, called *pahk kanah,* a sturdy Asian leafy vegetable sometimes translated as Asian kale. It's also good with *pahk kwahng-toong,* another member of the cabbage family that has small yellow flowers and is often available in Asian markets in the West. It is sometimes labeled *choy sum* or flowering bok choy. Any leafy vegetable in the cabbage family works well. You could also use spinach if you stir it in just before the dish is ready.

KWAYTIOW PAHT KI-MAO
Rice Noodles Stir-Fried with Fresh Chilies and Holy Basil

Hot green chilies and holy basil, *bai graprao* in Thai, make this dish hot stuff. Thais usually season their portions with the traditional Thai noodle condiments—crushed dried red chilies, sugar, fish sauce, and fresh hot chilies in white vinegar—but I love it just like this.

2 tablespoons coarsely chopped fresh kii noo, *serrano, or jalapeño chili*
1 tablespoon coarsely chopped garlic
1 tablespoon sugar
1/4 teaspoon salt
Freshly ground black pepper to taste
3 tablespoons fish sauce
1 teaspoon dark soy sauce
2 to 4 tablespoons vegetable oil
1/4 pound ground pork, beef, or turkey, or finely chopped chicken
1/2 pound soft, fresh rice noodle sheets, cut lengthwise into strips about 1 inch
 wide, or 3 cups dried rice noodles (1/2 inch wide), boiled until tender and drained
3/4 cup fresh graprao *basil leaves or other fresh basil leaves or mint leaves*
5 cherry tomatoes, quartered lengthwise

Place the chilies and garlic next to the stove. Combine the sugar, salt, and black pepper in one small bowl, and the fish sauce and soy sauce in another, and place these by the stove as well. Prepare all of the remaining ingredients and place them by the stove, along with a serving platter.

Heat a wok or large, deep skillet over medium-high heat. Add 2 tablespoons of the oil and swirl to coat the surface. When the oil is very hot, drop a piece of garlic into the pan. If it sizzles immediately, the oil is ready. Add the garlic and toss until golden, about 30 seconds. Add the chilies and toss for a further 30 seconds.

Add the pork and stir-fry, using a spatula to break up and brown the meat, 1 to 2 minutes. Add the sugar mixture and toss rapidly to mix. Add the fish sauce mixture and continue to stir-fry as the sauce bubbles and thickens slightly, about 1 minute.

Add the rice noodles and turn them over gently and repeatedly as they soften and absorb the sauce, about 1 minute. Add more oil if needed. Add most of the basil, reserving a few leaves for garnish, and continue turning gently until it begins to wilt. Add the tomatoes, turn once, and remove from the heat. Transfer the noodles to a serving platter and garnish with the remaining basil. Serve at once.

SERVES 2 TO 4.

MEE GROP
Crispy Rice Noodles

For this dish, the thinnest rice noodles *(sen mee)* are deep-fried to a light, crisp tangle, tossed in a piquant sweet-sour chili sauce, and garnished with pickled garlic, bean sprouts, green onion tops, and strips of red chili.

Even though I've given you a simplified recipe, it's still a tremendous amount of work to make this spectacular dish. A traditional version would include lacy nets of egg fried to a puffy golden brown, crisp-fried rods of pressed bean curd, dried shrimp, and the juice and zest of *som sah,* a particularly sour orange unavailable in the West. Originally *mee grop* did not include pork or fresh shrimp, relying on bean curd and dried shrimp instead, but these additions are common today.

Since *mee grop* is served at room temperature, it's a grand center-piece for a celebration meal. Thais prepare it in large quantities for the feasts accompanying weddings, Buddhist ordinations, moving into a new home, or celebrating a birth. Sweet and delicate and containing little meat, it's the kind of dish especially appropriate for serving to the monks who are invited to bless such occasions.

1/2 pound very thin, dried rice noodles
Vegetable oil for deep-frying
1/4 pound pork tenderloin, sliced into small, thin pieces
1/4 pound medium shrimp, peeled and deveined
1 tablespoon coarsely chopped garlic
2 tablespoons coarsely chopped shallot
2 tablespoons fish sauce
2 tablespoons white vinegar
1 tablespoon brown bean sauce (dao jiow)
1 teaspoon crushed dried red chilies
1/4 cup sugar
1/4 cup palm sugar or brown sugar
2 tablespoons freshly squeezed lime juice
3 cups bean sprouts
2 heads Pickled Garlic (page 183)
1 bunch garlic chives, or 9 medium green onions, cut into 1-inch lengths
5 fresh red chee fah chilies sliced crosswise on the diagonal into thin ovals, or a handful of long, thin sweet red pepper strips

Gently pull the dried rice noodles apart, breaking them into small handfuls 3 inches long. Set them aside in a heap. Tiny shards will fly around the room as you do this, so you could break them up inside a big grocery bag or just plan to sweep up after you're done. Select a utensil for removing batches of cooked noodles from the hot oil very quickly. A large, long-handled mesh scoop is ideal, or 2 long-handled slotted spoons will do. Place a large tray or 2 baking sheets beside the stove to hold the fried noodles; line the tray or sheets with paper towels. Have handy a large serving platter and 2 long-handled spoons or pasta forks for tossing the puffed noodles with the sauce.

Pour oil into a wok or large, deep skillet to a depth of 3 inches. Heat over medium heat to 325° to 350°F. Drop a piece of rice noodle into the pan. If it sinks and then floats and puffs immediately, the oil is ready.

Drop a small handful of the noodles into the oil. Turn them once and remove them as soon as they've swelled and changed color from ivory to white to a very faint golden brown. This takes seconds, so don't answer any phone calls until you're done. Hold the puffed noodles over the pan briefly to drain, and transfer to the towel-lined tray. Repeat this process until all the noodles are cooked.

Carefully pour off all but 2 tablespoons of the hot oil into another large pot and set aside to cool. Place the wok or skillet over medium heat for about 1 minute to heat the oil until very hot. Add the pork and stir-fry until it is no longer pink, about 2 minutes. Add the shrimp and stir-fry until they turn pink and are opaque and firm, 1 to 2 minutes. Using a slotted spoon, transfer the shrimp and pork to a small bowl and set aside.

To the same pan, add the garlic and toss until golden, about 30 seconds. Add the shallots, toss well, and then stir-fry until softened and aromatic, about 1 minute. Add the fish sauce, vinegar, bean sauce, dried chilies, and both sugars and bring to a gentle boil. Stir to dissolve sugar, mixing well. Cook the sauce gently until it resembles a thin, shiny syrup, 5 to 7 minutes. Add the lime juice, then taste and adjust seasoning for a pleasing balance of sweet, salty, and sour.

Reduce the heat to low, add the reserved pork and shrimp to the sauce, and stir once. Add half the rice noodles and, using 2 long-handled spoons or pasta forks, toss gently, mixing the noodles into the sauce. Add the remaining noodles and cook another 1 or 2 minutes, tossing gently to distribute sauce and separate clumps while breaking as few noodles as possible.

When noodles are fairly evenly coated, mound onto the serving platter, placing an appealing number of shrimp in full view. Pile the bean sprouts onto one end of the platter. Slice the garlic heads crosswise into thin rounds. Garnish the noodles with the garlic, garlic chives, and chili strips. Serve at room temperature.

SERVES 6 TO 8.

KANOME JEEN SAO NAHM
Rice Noodle Nests with Fresh Ginger, Dried Shrimp, Pineapple, Chilies, and Coconut Cream

Sao nahm means "to stir or rinse in water," a basic step in the process of making *kanome jeen,* the particular type of soft rice noodles used in this dish. But it says nothing about the lovely array of condiments that accompany this elegant version. Its rich coconut milk, great array of ingredients, and the absence of such prosaic accompaniments as bean sprouts, wild sour herbs, and sliced green beans marks it as a central Thai dish in the palace style. It's easy, too—just a bit of chopping and arranging to do while you cook the noodles and heat up the coconut cream. Since *kanome jeen* are a delicate rice noodle made fresh daily, they are very difficult to find in the West. The dried Japanese noodle *somen* is an excellent substitute and widely available.

1/2 pound dried somen *noodles or slender rice noodles*
Banana leaves for lining platter (optional)
2 cups coconut cream
1 small pineapple
1/2 cup very finely shredded, peeled fresh ginger
1/2 cup garlic cloves, thinly sliced lengthwise
2 limes, cut lengthwise into 8 wedges
1/2 cup dried shrimp, pounded to a very coarse powder or finely chopped
1/4 cup coarsely ground dried red chili
1/4 cup sugar
1/4 cup fish sauce
6 fresh kii noo *chilies, thinly sliced, or 1 tablespoon minced fresh serrano chilis*

Bring a large pot of water to an angry boil over high heat. Sprinkle in the noodles and stir a few times to separate them. Let them cook for about 3 minutes. Meanwhile, place a colander in the sink.

When the noodles are white and tender, pour them into the colander and let all of the water drain away. Quickly fill the cooking pot with cold tap water and drop the noodles into the pot, leaving it in the sink. Use your hands to separate the noodles and cool them down quickly and gently.

Place a large platter by the pot and line it with banana leaves if you like. Scoop out a handful of the noodles, let them drain a bit, and shape the hank into a little nest. Use about 1/2 cup of noodles per nest, and place the nests on the platter in overlapping circles. Continue until you have about 25 nests. Set aside at room temperature.

Pour the coconut cream into a small saucepan and place it over low heat until it is very hot and just beginning to boil.

Remove from the heat and let it cool while you prepare the condiments to accompany the noodles. Prepare the pineapple by chopping off the top and halving the fruit lengthwise. Pare away the thick peel on the outside of the pineapple, and then cut out the small brown eyes that remain. Cut each half lengthwise into quarters and cut off and discard the coarse core portion on each piece. Carefully slice these pieces into small, thin shreds, keeping as much juice as possible. Place 2 cups of the shredded pineapple in a bowl to serve with this noodle dish and enjoy any extra for a snack.

Place the ginger, garlic, limes, dried shrimp, dried chilies, and sugar in separate small bowls or saucers, or arrange them together in small mounds on a colorful plate. Transfer the coconut cream to a bowl. Pour the fish sauce into another bowl and sprinkle the fresh chilies on top.

To serve, have each diner put 2 or 3 noodle nests on a plate and sprinkle the condiments over the noodles to taste. Be sure everyone includes a nice drizzle of coconut cream and a squeeze of lime juice. Toss and eat, serving at room temperature.

SERVES 8.

NOTE: The noodles can also be served in a single large tangle in a shallow bowl, with the dry condiments sprinkled on top and the liquid condiments in small bowls alongside. To serve, pour the coconut cream, fish sauce, and lime juice over the noodles, toss well, and serve immediately.

KWAYTIOW NAHM GAI RUH BEHT
Rice Noodles in Stock with Roast Chicken or Roast Duck

In Thailand, soup noodles are a meal in a bowl. They're inexpensive, satisfying, and delicious, so you'll find vendors dishing them up wherever customers beckon. Thais eat noodles with chopsticks and a big spoon for the broth. Soup noodles are seldom spicy, but there is always a battery of condiments on hand to suit every palate: crushed dried red chilies, sugar, crushed peanuts, fish sauce, and white vinegar afloat with fresh chili slices.

6 cups Basic Chicken Stock (page 186)
1 pound soft, fresh rice noodle sheets, cut lengthwise into strips 3/4 inch wide, or
  wide, dried rice noodles, boiled until tender and drained
2 cups coarsely shredded roast chicken or roast duck, with skin left on
6 tablespoons fish sauce
1/2 cup thinly sliced green onion (sliced crosswise)
1/2 cup coarsely chopped fresh cilantro, including some stems
Freshly ground white or black pepper
1/2 cup Fried Garlic in Oil (page 184)

In a saucepan over medium heat, bring the chicken stock to a boil. Meanwhile, place a generous handful of fresh rice noodles into each individual serving bowl. Add a portion of the roast chicken or duck, a tablespoon of fish sauce, and a heaping tablespoon of green onions.

When the stock is hot, ladle 1 cup into each serving bowl. Add a sprinkling of cilantro leaves, a generous sprinkling of pepper, and a generous tablespoon of garlic and oil. Serve at once.

SERVES 6.

KIOW NAHM
Wonton Soup

This Chinese import is as popular in Thailand as it is in the West, and I think you'll love the Thai version. Like spring rolls, it takes a little time to make, but the delicious results are worth every minute. It's not complicated work, but there's assembly and a session of repetitious folding of the dumplings, so make it when you're not in a rush. If you can enlist a helper or two whose company you enjoy, it can be a very pleasant endeavor. And carefully made wonton soup is its own reward. If you go to the trouble to make this dish, you deserve to enjoy it Asian style, as a whole meal rather than just as a soup course.

FILLING
1/2 pound ground pork
1/2 pound shrimp, peeled, deveined, and finely chopped
2 tablespoons Cilantro Pesto (page 168)
1/4 teaspoon sugar
1/2 teaspoon salt

1 package (12 ounces) square wonton wrappers
6 cups Basic Chicken Stock (page 186)
1 1/2 cups small spinach leaves, left whole, or large leaves, torn into 2-inch pieces
4 to 6 tablespoons fish sauce
Freshly ground pepper
About 1/2 cup fresh cilantro leaves
4 to 6 tablespoons Fried Garlic in Oil (page 184)

To make the filling, combine the pork, shrimp, pesto, sugar, and salt in a large bowl. Mix everything together thoroughly. Hands work best for this step, but a large wooden or metal spoon will do. Prepare to fold the wontons by arranging the following things on a table where you can sit and work: the package of wonton wrappers, unopened; measuring spoons; a small bowl of water to use for sealing the wrappers closed; a cutting board on which to lay out the wrappers as you fill them; and large platters or trays where 50 or 60 folded wontons can rest without touching each other.

Begin by opening the wrapper package and placing a wrapper before you; cover the rest with a clean kitchen towel. Put about 1 teaspoon of filling in the center of the wrapper. Moisten the edges of the wrapper with a little water and fold the wrapper in half over the filling; press the edges together to seal it well. Then bring all the edges together under the filling, so that the filling makes a fat ball on top. Pinch the edges together, moistening them as needed to seal securely. Set the wonton aside on a platter and continue, working on 3 or 4 wontons at a time if you like. If the wontons touch each other or get wet, they will stick and tear open, so keep them separate and dry. Keep the unused wrappers covered while you work, as they dry out quickly. Seal up and freeze any leftover wrappers for another day.

To cook the wontons, bring about 2 quarts of water to a rolling boil in a large pot. Have handy about 3 cups of cold water and a 1-cup measure. Drop the wontons into the boiling water. As soon as it returns to a rolling boil, add 1 cup of the cold water. When the water boils again, add another cup of the cold water. When it boils a third time, add another cup of water. When the water returns to a boil this time, scoop out the wontons carefully with a slotted spoon and transfer them to a large bowl. Set the bowl aside while you prepare the soup. If the wontons stick together when you're ready for them, add a little cold water and separate them gently with your hands.

In a small saucepan over medium heat, bring the chicken stock to a boil. Set out large individual serving bowls and place 8 to 10 wontons in each bowl. Place a handful of spinach on one side of each wonton serving and carefully ladle about 1 cup of chicken stock into each bowl. Season each serving with about 1 tablespoon of fish sauce, a generous sprinkling of freshly ground pepper, a small handful of cilantro leaves, and about 1 teaspoon of fried garlic. Serve at once.

SERVES 4 TO 6.

NOTE: To save time, use canned chicken stock simmered for 10 minutes with 1/2 teaspoon freshly ground pepper and a handful of fresh cilantro, stems and all. Discard the cilantro before using the stock.

Uncooked wontons freeze beautifully, unless they're touching each other. Freeze them 1 inch apart on plates or trays, and then drop the frozen wontons into a plastic bag and seal tightly. Do not thaw the wontons before cooking them. Just drop the frozen wontons into boiling water, and allow 1 or 2 extra minutes of cooking if they need it.

BUA LOY
Floating Lotus Seeds

This sweet consists of plump dumplings of sticky rice flour, served bobbing in small bowls of warm, sweet coconut milk. To Thai people, the marble-sized dumplings resemble the seeds of the lotus, Buddhism's sacred flower, so that's how the sweet got its auspicious Thai name. The dish originated in China and appears with small variations throughout Southeast Asia. *Bua loy* is associated with celebration and good fortune, so you'll often find it served during the traditional family feasting that accompanies New Year's celebrations, weddings, and the ordination of Buddhist monks.

1 1/2 cups sticky rice flour
3/4 cup water
3 1/2 cups coconut milk
2 teaspoons salt
1/2 cup palm sugar or brown sugar
1/4 cup sugar

Fill a large saucepan with water and bring it to a rolling boil over high heat. Meanwhile, place the flour in a mixing bowl and slowly stir in the water. Use your fingers to form the mixture into a loose dough. Turn the dough onto a lightly floured surface and knead it until it is claylike and smooth. If the dough is dry and crumbly, add a little more water; if it's sticky and gooey, add more flour.

When the dough is ready, divide it into 4 equal portions. With the palms of the hands, roll each portion into a long, slender log about 3/4 inch thick. Cut each log into small pieces abut 1/2 inch thick, and then roll each piece between your palms into a smooth ball about the size of a marble. You will have around 100 dumplings.

Place a slotted spoon and a large bowl of cool water next to the pan of boiling water. To cook the dumplings, drop a batch of about 25 dough balls into the pot and boil until they float to the top, 1 to 2 minutes. Remove the floating dumplings with the slotted spoon and drop them into the bowl of cool water. Continue until all the dumplings are cooked.

In a small saucepan, combine the coconut milk, salt, and both sugars. Place over medium heat until the mixture reaches a gentle boil, 5 to 10 minutes. Stir occasionally to dissolve the sugar, salt, and any lumps of coconut cream. The mixture should not reach a vigorous boil. Remove from the heat and set aside to cool a little.

To serve, divide the rice flour dumplings among small serving bowls, placing about 15 dumplings in each bowl. Ladle about 1/2 cup of the warm coconut milk mixture over each serving, leaving the dumplings visible. They floated naturally while boiling in water, but they won't float now, so be sure to put enough dumplings in each serving bowl so that they appear to be floating in a pool of coconut milk.

SERVES 6 TO 8.

GLUAY BUAT CHEE
Bananas Stewed in Coconut Milk

When women in Thailand become Buddhist nuns, they wear white robes. This sweet dish of bananas in coconut milk is white as well, giving rise to its charming Thai name, "bananas ordained as nuns."

4 cups coconut milk
1 cup sugar
1 teaspoon salt
2 pounds bananas, preferably underripe

In a medium saucepan, combine the coconut milk, sugar, and salt. Place over medium heat until the mixture reaches a gentle boil, 5 to 10 minutes. Stir occasionally to dissolve the sugar, salt, and any lumps of coconut cream. The mixture should not reach a vigorous boil.

Meanwhile, peel the bananas, halve them lengthwise, and then cut them into 2-inch chunks. You should have about 4 cups of banana chunks. When the coconut milk reaches a gentle boil, add the bananas and cook until the mixture returns to the boil, 1 to 2 minutes. Remove from the heat and let cool in the saucepan. Serve in small bowls warm or at room temperature.

SERVES 6 TO 8.

NOTE: Thais make this homey sweet with *gluay nahm wah,* a short, chubby variety of banana that is much firmer than the variety commonly found in North America. If you have the chance to try this recipe with the traditional bananas, be sure to increase the cooking time until the bananas become soft.

I like to freeze any leftovers for a coconut-banana milkshake, which I make by combining the frozen leftovers with a little extra ice and any ripe fruit that I have on hand. Then I put everything into a blender and blend until it's a smooth, thick shake.

SOM LOY GAEO
Oranges in Chilled Syrup

This is a simple, cool fruit dessert, the perfect refreshment for a sultry summer afternoon. Prepare the syrup and oranges in advance, and then combine and ice them whenever you're ready to serve. Thais often scent the syrup with jasmine flower essence. If you can find some, add it after removing the syrup from the heat. You could use rose water or orange flower water as well.

1 1/2 cups sugar
3 cups water
5 oranges (about 2 1/2 pounds)
Crushed ice

Combine the sugar and water in a medium saucepan. Bring to a gentle boil over medium heat, stirring occasionally to dissolve the sugar. Boil gently until you have a thin, smooth, slightly golden syrup, 10 to 15 minutes. Remove from the heat, let cool to room temperature, cover, and chill.

Cut off the top and bottom of an orange to expose the flesh. Set the orange on a cutting board and, using a sharp knife, slice downward, following the curve of the orange, until all the peel and pith is removed. Loosen the meat by running a knife between the segments and separating them. Place the segments in a bowl. Repeat with the remaining oranges, adding the segments to the bowl as you work. Cover the bowl and chill the oranges well.

To serve, divide the chilled orange segments among small individual serving bowls and drizzle each portion with a generous amount of the chilled syrup. Add 2 or 3 tablespoons of crushed ice to each bowl and serve at once.

SERVES 4 TO 6.

KAO NIOW MAMUANG
Sticky Rice with Mangoes

Thailand in April is scorching and humid, and the only respite from the heat up-country is to take a lot of baths and a lot of naps. But when evening finally comes, vendors in night markets throughout the kingdom serve up a lovely reward for enduring the infernal heat—delicate yellow mangoes ripened to perfection by the merciless sun and paired with sticky rice kissed with sweet, rich coconut milk.

Unfortunately the pale green, slender *oke loeng* mango, which Thais serve with sticky rice, isn't available in the West. But this dessert is still wonderful with the mangoes we can get here. You could also serve it with a rainbow of the sweetest, ripest fruit you can find—peaches, nectarines, plums, kiwi fruits, strawberries, bananas.

You must plan to make this dish in advance, as the rice is soaked for three hours before cooking and the cooked rice then needs time to cool to room temperature.

Sticky Rice in Sweet-Salty Coconut Cream (page 166)
6 ripe, sweet mangoes or any ripe, sweet fruit (about 1 1/2 cups sliced per person)

Prepare the coconut rice and set it aside to cool to room temperature.

Shortly before serving, peel and slice the mangoes, removing as much meat as you can in large, tender pieces. Avoid cutting very close to the seed where the meat is fibrous. For each serving, arrange a fist-sized portion of coconut rice on a dessert or salad plate, along with several slices of mango or other fruit. Serve at room temperature.

SERVES 6.

NOTE: The cooked rice will keep for 6 to 8 hours. Do not refrigerate it or it will harden.

The sticky rice in this dish is traditionally garnished with a sprinkling of tiny, crunchy toasted *tua tohng,* which means "gold beans." These are the tiny yellow centers of mung beans, often available in Asian markets in small bags. If you'd like to try them, dry-fry them in a skillet over medium heat, shaking the pan often, until they are lightly browned, 5 to 10 minutes. Sprinkle them over the rice just before serving.

Mangoes seem to be about one-third seed, and there's a lot of heavenly sweet fruit too fibrous to cut off and enjoy delicately in polite company. For this reason, I strongly suggest you retire to the kitchen with only your dearest friends and family, lean over the sink, and gnaw on the meaty mango seeds with messy, joyous abandon.

KAO NIOW NAH GOONG
Sticky Rice with Shrimp, Coconut, and Wild Lime Leaves

In Thailand this sweet-savory dish is an elegant snack. The sticky rice is enriched with sweet coconut cream, and during the sweltering April heat it is served with sweet, ripe mangoes. When mango season is over, Thais enjoy the luxurious rice with this unusual topping of minced shrimp sautéed with cilantro, peppercorns, garlic, and freshly grated coconut. It's usually offered along with several other toppings, including the palm sugar custard called *sahngkayah* (page 70). In Thailand I often bought this dish from a specialty sweets vendor, who wrapped it in a little banana-leaf pyramid. Here I buy frozen banana leaves, cut them to line a serving platter, and place small mounds of coconut sticky rice on the lined platter. Then I crown each mound with the shrimp-coconut mixture or with a spoonful of the custard.

Thai cooks traditionally color this treat with a tiny bit of red food coloring and ground turmeric, to give it an appealing red-orange hue. Experiment with adding color to some extra grated coconut before you begin the recipe. When you know how much color you need, color the coconut you'll be using and start cooking. Also, be sure to allow yourself enough time to soak, cook, and cool the rice before assembling the dish.

Sticky Rice in Sweet-Salty Coconut Cream (page 166)
3 tablespoons vegetable oil
1 tablespoon Cilantro Pesto (page 168)
1/2 pound shrimp, peeled, deveined, and finely chopped
1 cup freshly grated coconut (page 180)
1/4 cup sugar
2 teaspoons salt
6 fresh wild lime leaves, sliced crosswise into very thin strips, or a handful of fresh cilantro leaves

Prepare the coconut rice first and set it aside to cool to room temperature.

Heat the oil in a small skillet over low heat until it is quite warm. Add the pesto and stir-fry as it sizzles gently, about 1 minute. Add the shrimp and stir-fry until they turn pink and are opaque, about 1 minute. Stir in the coconut. Add the sugar and salt and continue cooking, stirring occasionally, until the salt and sugar are dissolved and absorbed and the mixture is fairly dry, about 2 minutes. Remove from the heat and let cool to room temperature.

To serve, divide the coconut sticky rice into mounds the size of a small scoop of ice cream and place them on a serving platter. Place a tablespoon of shrimp-coconut mixture on the top of each mound and sprinkle it with a few strips of lime leaf. Serve at room temperature.

SERVES 4 TO 6.

SAHNGKAYAH
Steamed Custard

> *Sahngkayah* is a simple, traditional dessert, made with equal amounts of duck eggs, palm sugar, and coconut cream. You can substitute chicken eggs and brown sugar if you like, although the palm sugar imparts a deep country flavor that is quintessentially Thai.
>
> Because of its sweet richness, *sahngkayah* is seldom eaten "neat." It's steamed in something shallow, such as a cake pan or pie tin, and served in small spoonfuls atop mounds of *kao niow mun,* which is sticky rice softened with a bit of sweet-salty coconut cream (page 179).

3 duck eggs or 4 chicken eggs (about 1 cup shelled)
1 cup palm sugar or brown sugar
1 cup coconut cream

Fill a wok or a steamer pan with water, cover, and bring to a rolling boil over high heat. When the water boils, reduce the heat to low until you are ready to steam the custard.

Meanwhile, in a medium bowl, beat the eggs well with a fork or whisk. Add the sugar, stirring gently at first. If there are lumps of sugar, strain them out with a fork, mash them smooth with a fork or spoon, and return them to the egg mixture. When the mixture is smooth, thick, and well blended, add the coconut cream and beat gently. You will have about 2 1/2 cups of liquid.

Pour the liquid into an 8- or 9-inch cake pan or pie tin, or divide it among small custard cups or ramekins. Carefully place the custard on the steaming rack over the simmering water. Cover the cake pan or cups with a paper towel to prevent steam from dripping in. Increase the heat to maintain a strong head of steam and cover the pan. Begin timing now and steam until the custard puffs up a little and is quite firm and set around the edges, about 30 minutes. The center may still jiggle somewhat after it is done.

Turn off the heat and remove the cover, taking care to keep any steam that has condensed inside the cover from dripping into the custard. Leave the custard in the steamer to cool to room temperature, or remove it very carefully and set it aside to cool.

Serve at room temperature or chilled. The custard can be covered and refrigerated for 2 or 3 days.

SERVES 10 TO 12.

SAHNGKAYAH FAHK TONG
Custard Steamed in a Pumpkin

The sweet, rich Thai custard of eggs, palm sugar, and coconut cream is especially appealing when steamed in a small kabocha pumpkin. The soft pumpkin is a pleasing foil for the honey-colored, silky custard.

If possible, select a pumpkin with a nice stem. This will come in handy as a handle if you decide to steam the top along with the custard and set it on top for presentation. You could also use four to six acorn squashes, or another squat winter squash, as long as you can trim the base to make it stand upright for steaming and serving.

Liquid custard for Steamed Custard (page 70)
1 small kabocha pumpkin (1 to 2 pounds)

Prepare the recipe for Steamed Custard up to the point when you are ready to steam. You will have almost 2 1/2 cups of liquid custard; set aside.

Carefully cut out the top of the pumpkin, as you would to carve a jack-o'-lantern for Halloween. Try not to pierce the pumpkin at any other point with the knife, as it's more likely to crack or leak around such punctures. Using a large spoon or an ice cream scoop, scrape out and discard all the fibers and seeds.

Fill a wok or a steamer pan with water, cover, and bring to a rolling boil over high heat. Reduce the heat to low. Place the pumpkin on a plate that will fit nicely on the rack of the steamer or on a steaming rack inside the wok. Place the plate in the steamer over the simmering water and carefully pour the liquid custard into the pumpkin, filling to within 1 inch of the top. If you have extra liquid custard, steam it in custard cups or a small, shallow pan. Set the pumpkin top on the steamer rack as well, if you like. Cover the pumpkin and other custard containers with paper towels to prevent condensed steam from dripping in. Increase the heat to produce an active head of steam, then adjust the heat to maintain a steady, gentle steam and cover the pan. Begin timing now and steam until the custard puffs up a little and is firm on the surface, jiggling only slightly in the center, 45 minutes to 1 hour.

Turn off the heat and remove the cover, taking care to keep any steam that has condensed inside the cover from dripping into the custard. Leave the custard in the steamer to cool to room temperature, or remove it very carefully and set it aside to cool.

Serve at room temperature or chilled. Cut the pumpkin into thick wedges for serving.

SERVES 8 TO 10.

FAHK TONG GAENG BUAT
Pumpkin Stewed in Coconut Milk

This easy dessert is a pleasing East-West comfort food. Thais enjoy it as a sweet snack throughout the year, but since it's served warm and uses pumpkin, I like it as my breakfast or dessert on a chilly winter's day.

3 cups coconut milk
1 teaspoon salt
1/2 cup palm sugar or brown sugar
1/2 cup sugar
1 kabocha pumpkin, or other sturdy winter squash (about 2 pounds)
1 cup coconut cream

In a medium saucepan, combine the coconut milk, salt, and both sugars. Place over medium heat, bring to a gentle boil, and simmer 5 to 10 minutes. Stir occasionally to dissolve the sugars, salt, and any lumps of coconut cream suspended in the milk. Remove from the heat and set aside while you prepare the pumpkin.

Wash the pumpkin well, since you will peel off only part of the skin. Quarter the pumpkin lengthwise and cut away all of the stem. Scrape out and discard all the fibers and seeds. Cut each quarter lengthwise into 4 quarters and peel off most of the green skin. Then cut the pumpkin into pieces about 2 inches long and 1/2 inch thick.

Add the pumpkin pieces to the coconut milk mixture and bring it back to a gentle boil over medium heat. Do not stir, or you may mash the pumpkin pieces, which should remain whole and firm. Cook until they are tender but not very soft, 5 to 10 minutes. Add the coconut cream, bring to a gentle boil once more, and remove from the heat.

Serve warm in small bowls.

SERVES 6 TO 8.

KAH-FE YEN
Thai Iced Coffee with Milk

> *Kah-fe yen,* or "cold coffee," is made from a Thai-Chinese ground coffee powder. The powder is widely available in Asian markets, usually labeled as Thai coffee or *oliang* powder. Its distinctive, almost burnt flavor comes from the ground roasted sesame seed and corn that are mixed with the ground coffee beans.

4 cups water
1/4 cup Thai coffee powder
1 1/2 cups Sugar Syrup (page 187)
Crushed ice or ice cubes to fill each glass
1 to 1 1/2 cups evaporated milk or half-and-half (3 to 4 tablespoons per glass)

In a large, deep saucepan, bring the water to a rolling boil over medium heat. Stir in the coffee powder and return to a rolling boil. Immediately remove the pan from the heat and set it aside to cool. When the coffee reaches room temperature, strain it through a fine-mesh strainer or a coffee filter into a pitcher. Add the syrup and stir to dissolve. Cover and chill until serving time.

To serve, fill 4 to 6 tall glasses with ice. Add about 3/4 cup of the chilled coffee to each glass. Top off each glass with 3 to 4 tablespoons evaporated milk. Serve as the milk cascades over the ice and swirls into the coffee.

SERVES 4 TO 6.

> NOTE: Thais like their *kah-fe yen* very sweet, but you can decrease the amount of the syrup to taste. The coffee-syrup mixture will keep in the refrigerator for up to 1 week.

CHA YEN
Thai Iced Tea

In America's Thai restaurants, this cool, sweet treat converts many a timid first-timer to a Thai food fanatic on the spot. *Cha yen,* or "cold tea," is made from a special Thai blend of chopped black tea leaves flavored and perfumed with star anise, cinnamon, vanilla, and other sweet spices. A little food coloring gives it its signature terra-cotta hue. It is sold in Asian markets in 1-pound bags, usually labeled Thai tea or *cha Thai.* In Thailand it is only served cold and supersweet, crowned with a luxurious cloud of evaporated milk floating on the ice.

4 cups water
3/4 cup Thai tea
1 1/2 cups Sugar Syrup (page 187)
Crushed ice or ice cubes to fill each glass
1 to 1 1/2 cups evaporated milk or half-and-half (3 to 4 tablespoons per glass)

In a medium saucepan, bring the water to a rolling boil, and place a heatproof 1-quart pitcher in the sink. When the water boils, add the tea and remove the pan from the heat. The tea will float to the top until you stir gently to coax it into the water. When all of the tea leaves are wet, let steep for 3 minutes.

Pour the contents of the saucepan into the pitcher, and don't worry if the dregs are left behind. Pour the tea back and forth between the pitcher and saucepan 7 times as it becomes darker and stronger, ending up with the tea in the saucepan. Rinse out the pitcher and strain the tea through a coffee filter back into the pitcher. Add the syrup and stir to dissolve. Cool to room temperature, cover, and chill until serving time.

To serve, fill tall glasses with crushed ice. Add 3/4 cup of the chilled Thai tea per glass. Top off each glass with 3 to 4 tablespoons evaporated milk. Serve as the milk cascades over the ice and swirls into the tea.

SERVES 4 TO 6.

NOTE: Thais like their tea very sweet, but you can decrease the amount of syrup to taste. The tea-syrup mixture will keep in the refrigerator for 1 week.

GLUAY BAHN
Banana Smoothie

Gluay bahn is street food, a recent addition to Thai cuisine since it requires a *krueng bahn,* or "electric blender," to buzz everything into heavenly refreshing smoothness. Watermelon, pineapple, mango, or strawberries can be used too, and the riper the fruit, the better the smoothie.

2 cups ripe banana chunks
1/2 cup water
2 tablespoons Sugar Syrup (page 187) or honey
12 ice cubes (about 1 1/2 cups)

In the order given, combine all of the ingredients in the jar of a blender. Blend at high speed until smooth, about 30 seconds. Serve at once.

SERVES 2.

NAHM MENOW
Limeade

I grew up on my grandmother's fresh-squeezed lemonade, so when I learned that limeade was a standard summer cooler in Thailand I felt right at home. I was startled by my first sip, however, because Thais season their limeade with salt. In Thai language class we new Peace Corps volunteers learned to say *mai sai gleua*—"hold the salt"—but after a while I came to enjoy the limeade Thai style, with the flavor counterpoints of sweet, sour, and salt. This recipe is for unsalted limeade, so if you want yours Thai style, just stir about 1/4 teaspoon salt into your frosty glass.

1/2 cup freshly squeezed lime juice, including pulp (about 4 limes)
1 cup Sugar Syrup (page 187)
6 cups water
Ice cubes

Combine the lime juice, syrup, and water in a large pitcher and stir well. Taste, and add more syrup or lime juice if you like. Cover and chill.

Serve in tall glasses over ice.

SERVES 6.

PAHK NEUA
The North

Northern Thailand is cool and green, with teak forests and rolling mountains stretching from the town of Tak to the rivers that mark the borders of Burma and Laos. It's no surprise that both these neighboring countries have a considerable impact on northern Thai culture and cuisine.

For a taste of Burmese influence, try *gaeng hahng ley*, a pork-ginger curry, or *kao soi*, a bowl of egg noodles in a delicious coconut curry of chicken or beef. Both use the traditional Burmese seasoning of ginger, dried chilies, onion, and turmeric, and are only mildly hot.

Also present here is the culinary tradition of the Thai-Yai, or Shan people, who came from China to settle in northern Thailand and the northeastern states of Burma. Two Thai-Yai dishes have become synonymous with northern Thai food, and both are rich sauces of minced pork sautéed with onions, tomato, and dried chilies. *Nahm prik ohng* is a dipping sauce with raw vegetables and crispy pork skins, and *kanome jeen nahm ngiow* is a similar sauce served over noodles with crispy garlic and pickled Chinese cabbage.

Many northern dishes use *tua nao*, small, thin disks of fermented soybeans, similar to the salty, Chinese brown bean sauce called *dao jiow* but in dried, portable form. The leathery, dark brown pancakes are toasted and then crumbled or pounded. They're not widely available outside northern Thailand, much less in the West, but either *dao jiow* or shrimp paste makes a good substitute if you bear in mind that both are saltier than *tua nao*.

Lao-style dishes abound in northern cuisine, and, like the Laotians, northern Thais eat sticky rice at every meal. *Nahm prik noom* is a chunky chili sauce served as a pungent dip with fresh vegetables. Its sharp chili-lime flavor is fortified by the roasting of the chilies, tomatoes, onions, and garlic, a Lao technique used in the *jaew* dipping sauces also popular in the northeast. *Ook gai* is a country-style red chicken curry enhanced with stalks of fresh lemongrass. The simple mushroom stir-fry called *paht heht* is another dish popular in Laos, with its mushroom-rich forests, and *kao taen* is a northern Thai version of Laotian puffed rice cakes swirled with caramelized palm sugar.

Northern Thai hospitality is legendary, so as you cook these recipes imagine yourself a guest in a traditional northern house, a large teak structure built on posts. You're warmly welcomed and offered a refreshing drink on your arrival, and ushered to a *khan toke* table, a small, low round table made of teak or lacquer. You sit on beautiful woven mats on the floor around the table with your hosts and other guests.

First you'll receive a serving of sticky rice. The rice is finger food, as are most of the dishes awaiting you in small bowls on the table. A traditional meal might include *gaeng hahng ley*, *nahm prik ohng*, *ook gai*, and *lahp*, a Lao-style dish equally popular in northeastern Thailand. Your meal might conclude with fresh fruit and a round of tiny, Burmese-style cigars, amid bouquets of smiles, laughter, and charming conversation in Pasah Peun Meuang—the delicate dialect of northern Thailand.

NAHM PRIK OHNG
Spicy Minced Pork Sauce with Raw Vegetables

> *Nahm prik ohng* is a regional dish whose popularity extends to all parts of Thailand. A tasty meat sauce studded with tomatoes and onions, it's traditionally served in a small bowl along with raw vegetables, crisp-fried pork skins, and sticky rice, all of which are dipped into the moderately spicy sauce.

Sticky Rice (page 165)
7 to 10 small dried red chilies
1/2 teaspoon salt
1 piece fermented soybean cake (tua nao), *lightly toasted, or 1/2 teaspoon shrimp paste*
2 tablespoons coarsely chopped shallot
1 tablespoon coarsely chopped garlic
1 tablespoon vegetable oil
1/4 pound coarsely chopped pork
20 cherry tomatoes, cut lengthwise into eighths
1 tablespoon fish sauce
1 teaspoon brown sugar
2 small cucumbers, peeled and sliced on the diagonal into thick ovals
7 green beans, trimmed and halved crosswise
2 wedges green cabbage (about 2 inches wide at widest point)
Crisp-fried pork skins

Prepare the rice, allowing at least 4 hours for soaking and cooking.

Meanwhile, stem the chilies and shake out and discard most of the seeds. Cut the chilies into small pieces and soak the pieces in warm water to cover for 20 minutes. Drain the chilies and transfer to a large, heavy mortar. Add the salt and pound and grind with a pestle until the chilies are broken down, about 3 minutes. Crumble the soybean cake into the mortar, then add the shallot and garlic. Pound to work the mixture into a paste, about 5 minutes. Pound more judiciously now, keeping the mortar well in front of you to avoid nasty splashes of chili goo, and using a spoon to scrape the ingredients together now and then. When you have a coarse, rust-colored purée, set it aside.

Heat a wok or deep, heavy medium skillet over low heat for 1 minute. Add the oil and swirl to coat the surface. Warm the oil for 1 minute. Add the chili paste and cook for 3 minutes, scraping and turning now and then, until it is fragrant and the color darkens a little.

Increase the heat to medium and crumble in the pork. Add the tomatoes, toss a few times, and simmer until the tomatoes wilt and the sauce reddens and thickens, 3 or 4 minutes. Stir in the fish sauce and sugar and simmer another 2 minutes. Taste and adjust seasoning for a pleasing balance of salty, hot, sour, and sweet. Remove from the heat and let the sauce cool.

To serve, transfer the sauce to a small bowl and place it on a platter along with the cucumbers, green beans, cabbage wedges, and pork skins. Serve warm or at room temperature with the rice.

SERVES 4.

NOTE: You can grind the chili paste in a small blender or food processor. Combine the chilies, salt, shallots, garlic, and soybean cake and grind until fairly smooth, adding a little water as needed.

For a simpler version, substitute 1 tablespoon prepared red curry paste for the chilies, salt, shallot, garlic, and soybean cake. And, yes, you can omit the pork skins.

NAHM PRIK NOOM
Roasted Banana Pepper Dipping Sauce with Fresh Vegetables

For this robust, northern-style sauce, pale green or yellow banana peppers are roasted with shallots, garlic, and tomatoes and pounded to an aromatic purée with salted mackerel and lime juice. The vegetables listed as accompaniments are traditional, but you can make a quick version with just cucumbers, beans, and cabbage. A simple, country-style meal would mate *nahm prik noom* with pork spareribs or grilled fish, a Thai omelet, and sticky rice.

9 *fresh* yuak *chilies (banana peppers or Hungarian wax peppers)*
9 *garlic cloves, unpeeled*
6 *shallots, unpeeled and halved lengthwise*
6 *cherry tomatoes*
2 *tablespoons vegetable oil*
3 *small salted mackerel* (plah too)
2 *tablespoons fish sauce*
2 *tablespoons freshly squeezed lime juice*
1 *tablespoon water*
1 *teaspoon sugar*
6 *green beans, trimmed, halved crosswise, blanched 1 minute, and drained*
1/2 *cup kabocha pumpkin or acorn squash chunks, boiled until tender and drained*
1/2 *cup well-drained canned baby corn, or fresh baby corn, trimmed, blanched 1 minute, and drained*
2 *wedges green cabbage (about 2 inches wide at widest point)*
2 *small cucumbers, peeled and sliced on the diagonal into thick ovals*

Prepare a hot fire in a charcoal grill or preheat a gas grill or a broiler until very hot. Roast the chilies, garlic, shallots, and tomatoes for about 10 minutes, turning occasionally, until they are softened and somewhat charred but not burnt. Place them on small bamboo skewers or on a fine-mesh screen if needed to keep them from falling through the grill grate. Remove and set aside to cool.

Heat the oil in a small skillet over medium heat for 1 minute. Add the mackerel and fry until golden, turning once, 4 to 6 minutes. Transfer to a small plate and set aside.

Stem and seed the roasted peppers; remove some of the blackened skin. Coarsely chop the peppers and transfer them to a large mortar. Peel the garlic and shallots and remove and discard roots. Coarsely chop and add to the mortar. Pound until a coarse purée forms. Carefully quarter the roasted tomatoes and add them, with their seeds and juice, to the mortar. Remove the meat from 1 fried mackerel, break the meat into small chunks, and add it to the mortar. Gently grind the tomatoes and fish into the chili sauce until a coarse puree forms. Add the fish sauce, lime juice, water, and sugar and stir well. Taste and adjust seasonings to your liking. Transfer to a small serving bowl.

Arrange the following on a large serving platter around the bowl of roasted chili sauce: 2 fried mackerel, the green beans, pumpkin, baby corn, cucumber, and cabbage. Serve at room temperature.

SERVES 4 TO 6.

NOTE: You can dry-fry the chili, garlic, shallots, and tomatoes in a small, heavy skillet over medium heat instead of roasting them. Halve the chilies lengthwise and then crosswise first, so there will be more surface exposed to the heat, and turn the vegetables frequently, cooking 10 to 15 minutes until they are aromatic and lightly charred.

If you don't have a large mortar and pestle, chop the ingredients very fine before adding them to a bowl, and then mash them well with a fork or the back of a spoon to make a coarse paste.

KANOME JEEN NAHM NGIOW
Rice Noodles with Spicy Minced Pork Sauce, Thai-Yai Style

Like *nahm prik ohng,* this dish comes from the Thai-Yai people, who migrated into northern Thailand and Burma from southern China centuries ago. It's a hearty minced pork–tomato sauce over rice noodles with crisp-fried garlic and green onions. Preparing the sauce takes a little time, but once you're done it's a good dish to serve buffet style for a large group.

Two types of rice noodles are traditionally used for this dish. One is *kwaytiow sen lek,* a thin, flat rice noodle, available dried in Asian markets. The other is *kanome jeen,* a delicate, spaghettilike noodle that is made fresh daily and difficult to find in the West. The dried Japanese wheat noodle called *somen* is a good substitute.

2 pounds pork spareribs
5 cups water
1 tablespoon vegetable oil
3 tablespoons Red Curry Paste (page 171)
1 teaspoon ground turmeric
1 pound finely minced pork
20 cherry tomatoes, halved lengthwise
1 tablespoon brown bean sauce (dao jiow)
1 tablespoon fish sauce
1 tablespoon freshly squeezed lime juice
1 pound dried slender rice noodles or somen
1/2 cup Fried Garlic in Oil (page 184), drained of oil
A handful of fresh cilantro leaves
1/2 cup thinly sliced green onions (sliced crosswise)
2 cups bean sprouts
1 lime, cut lengthwise into 8 wedges

Place the spareribs and the water in a large saucepan and bring to a boil over medium heat. When the water boils, reduce the heat to maintain a visible simmer; skim off any foam that rises to the top. Simmer until meat is very tender, 30 minutes. Remove the pan from the heat and set aside to cool.

Heat a wok or large, deep skillet over medium heat. Add the oil and swirl to coat the surface. When the oil is hot, add the curry paste, tumeric, and minced pork. Stir for 1 minute to break up the meat and mix it with the curry paste. Reduce the heat to maintain an active simmer and cook until the pork has changed color and the curry paste is fragrant, about 5 minutes. Add the tomatoes, simmer for 5 more minutes, and remove from the heat.

Meanwhile, remove the spareribs from their cooking liquid with a slotted spoon, reserving the liquid. Pull the meat from the bones, discarding the bones. Chop the meat coarsely and return it to the soup. Add the minced pork–tomato mixture and stir it in well. Combine the bean sauce, fish sauce, and lime juice in a small bowl. Mash with a fork or spoon to form a coarse paste. Add to the pot, stir well, and bring to a gentle boil over medium heat. Simmer for 1 minute, then taste to see that it has a nice salty-sour balance. Adjust as needed with fish sauce or lime juice. Cover and keep warm.

Bring a large pot of water to a rolling boil over high heat. Add the noodles and cook until just done, tossing to separate them as they cook, about 5 minutes. Drain, toss briefly under cold running water, and transfer to a large serving platter.

Pour about half of the warm sauce over the center of the noodles; pour the remaining sauce into a small serving bowl. Sprinkle the noodles with the fried garlic, cilantro, and green onions. Place the bean sprouts, lime wedges, and bowl of remaining sauce on a small plate. Toss the noodles and serve in individual plates or bowls, offering bean sprouts, lime wedges, and additional sauce on the side. Serve hot or warm.

SERVES 6 TO 8.

NOTE: This dish works well as part of a buffet. Prepare the sauce and its accompaniments in advance and reheat gently just before serving time. Cook the noodles and set up your ingredients as a noodle vendor would in Thailand: Set out separate containers of noodles, sauce, fried garlic, green onions, cilantro leaves, lime wedges, and bean sprouts. Provide guests with plates or bowls and have them help themselves.

Traditionally, fried whole dried red chilies and thinly sliced pickled Chinese cabbage, such as Tientsin pickled vegetable, are offered as accompaniments along with the bean sprouts and lime wedges. For the chilies, fry them in medium-hot vegetable oil until they darken slightly. Drain the pickled cabbage and shred it into very thin strips.

Any cooked noodles may be substituted for the rice noodles or somen.

GAENG HAHNG LEY
Burmese-Style Pork Curry with Fresh Ginger

This popular curry has many hallmarks of northern Thai cooking: the use of pork instead of chicken or beef, water rather than coconut milk, and brown sugar in place of palm sugar, and the inclusion of fresh ginger and turmeric. It's delicious and only moderately hot, and it improves greatly in flavor if made in advance and gently reheated. Many Thais enjoy the richness of fresh bacon, and I do too, but it's fine to substitute additional pork instead, and to use a lean cut instead of a fatty one.

1/4 cup finely slivered, peeled fresh ginger
12 small dried red chilies
3 tablespoons thinly sliced fresh lemongrass (sliced crosswise)
2 teaspoons finely diced fresh galanga
1 tablespoon shrimp paste
1/4 cup brown sugar
1 pound pork, with some fat attached
1/4 pound fresh bacon (pork belly)
2 1/2 cups water
2 teaspoons ground turmeric
1 teaspoon dark soy sauce
1/4 cup thinly sliced shallot (sliced lengthwise)
2 tablespoons minced garlic
2 tablespoons Tamarind Liquid (page 185)

Place the ginger in a small bowl. Add warm water just to cover and set aside. Stem the chilies. Coarsely chop the chilies into large pieces, and then transfer the chili pieces, seeds and all, to a large mortar. Add the lemongrass and galanga. Pound the ingredients until they form a coarse paste, scraping down the sides with a spoon as you go.

Add the shrimp paste and continue pounding until it is worked in well. Add the brown sugar and grind it in well, giving you a dark brown, grainy purée. Set the purée aside while you prepare the meat.

Cut both kinds of pork into large chunks. Place the meat in a large, heavy-bottomed saucepan and add the curry paste. Stir to coat the meat thoroughly with the paste. Then place the saucepan over low heat and let it heat up. In about 10 minutes the seasoned meat will begin to hiss and steam. Stir now and then, until all the meat has changed color and rendered some of its fat, and the curry paste is fragrant, about 10 minutes.

In a large measuring cup or a bowl, stir together the water, turmeric, and soy sauce and add them to the pot. Simmer over low heat until the meat is tender and is surrounded by a puddle of dark, thick, smooth sauce, about 40 minutes.

Add the shallot and garlic to the simmering curry. Drain the soaking ginger and add the soaking water to the pan. Place the soaked ginger in a mortar and gently pound it just to soften its fibers a little, but stopping before it loses its shape. Add the ginger to the curry and stir to mix everything together well.

Add the tamarind and taste the curry to see that it has a balance of flavors: salty, sour, and sweet. Adjust with tamarind, sugar, and fish sauce as needed. Cook just long enough to heat through, then remove from the heat. Let stand for 20 minutes and serve warm.

SERVES 6.

OOK GAI
Country-Style Chicken Curry with Lemongrass

This moderately hot curry is made with stock or water instead of coconut milk, and includes chunks of fresh lemongrass and wild lime leaves for a citrusy note. Serve it with lots of sticky rice.

10 to 12 small dried red chilies
5 stalks fresh lemongrass
1 teaspoon salt
1 tablespoon minced fresh galanga or ginger
1 tablespoon coarsely chopped cilantro root
2 tablespoons coarsely chopped garlic
2 tablespoons coarsely chopped shallot
1 teaspoon shrimp paste
1 teaspoon ground turmeric
2 tablespoons vegetable oil
6 chicken thighs (about 1 1/2 pounds), boned and cut into large chunks
3 cups chicken stock
2 tablespoons fish sauce
3 stalks fresh lemongrass
12 fresh wild lime leaves

Stem the chilies and shake out and discard most of the seeds. Cut the chilies into small pieces and soak the pieces in warm water to cover for 20 minutes.

Meanwhile, trim the 5 lemongrass stalks. Cut away and discard the grassy tops of each stalk, leaving 2 stalks 3 inches long and 3 stalks 6 inches long. Cut away any hard root section to leave a clean, smooth, flat base at the root end below the bulb. Remove and discard tough outer leaves. Thinly slice the 3-inch stalks crosswise and then finely mince. Place in a large, heavy mortar. Set the other 3 stalks aside.

Drain the chilies and add to the mortar with the salt. Pound and grind with a pestle until the chilies are broken down, about 5 minutes. Add the galanga, cilantro root, garlic, and shallot and grind and pound for 5 to 10 minutes until a coarse paste forms. Add the shrimp paste and turmeric and pound for about 3 minutes more. Set aside.

In a large saucepan, warm the oil over medium heat for 30 seconds. Add the curry paste and stir-fry, mashing it into the oil, until it is well blended, fragrant, and shiny, about 3 minutes. Add the chicken and stir-fry until it is lightly browned and coated with the paste, 3 to 5 minutes. Add the chicken stock and fish sauce and let the curry come to a boil.

Using the blunt edge of a cleaver blade or large knife, whack each of the 6-inch lemongrass stalks firmly at 2-inch intervals, rolling them over to bruise the stalks on all sides. Cut each stalk into 2-inch lengths and add to the curry along with 6 of the lime leaves. When the mixture reaches a boil, reduce the heat and simmer until chicken is cooked, about 20 minutes. Remove from the heat and stir in the remaining 6 lime leaves. Transfer to a serving bowl and serve.

SERVES 6 TO 8.

NOTE: Traditionally this curry is made with chunks of chicken with the bone left in. To prepare it in that manner, use a meat cleaver to chop the chicken into 1- or 2-inch chunks, and use water in place of chicken stock. You could also add the bones to the curry along with the boned meat, and remove them before serving. Thais usually use dark meat for long cooking because it has more flavor and becomes tender, but you can use breast meat if you prefer.

The curry paste can be ground in a small blender or food processor with a little of the chicken stock, instead of pounding in a mortar. Or, for speed, use 2 tablespoons prepared red curry paste and 1 teaspoon ground turmeric.

PAHT HEHT
Sautéed Mushrooms with Pork and White Pepper

I was given this simple, delicious recipe by Mrs. Wongkiow, an excellent home cook in Thailand's northernmost province of Chiang Rai. She prepares it with *heht nahng lome* (oyster mushrooms), or *heht fahng* (fresh straw mushrooms), both of which are readily available in Thailand. I make it with the beautiful dove-gray oyster mushrooms I sometimes find in Asian markets here, or even with the more common button mushrooms.

2 tablespoons vegetable oil
2 tablespoons thinly sliced garlic (sliced crosswise)
2 tablespoons finely slivered shallot, (slivered lengthwise)
1 small onion, thinly sliced lengthwise (about 1/2 cup)
1/4 pound pork, sliced into thin strips
1/2 pound fresh mushrooms, cut lengthwise into bite-sized pieces
2 tablespoons fish sauce
3 tablespoons water
1/2 teaspoon freshly ground white pepper

Heat a wok or large, deep skillet over medium-high heat. Add the oil and swirl to coat the surface. When the oil is very hot, drop a piece of the garlic into the pan. If it sizzles immediately, the oil is ready. Add the garlic and stir-fry until fragrant and golden, about 30 seconds. Add the shallot and stir-fry until it begins to wilt and becomes translucent, about 1 minute. Add the pork and stir-fry until it is no longer pink, about 2 minutes.

Add the mushrooms, toss to coat them with the oil, and cook for 1 minute. When they glisten and begin to soften, add the fish sauce, water, and pepper, and toss to combine. Stir-fry for 1 minute. Transfer to a serving platter and serve hot.

SERVES 4.

NOTE: You can substitute any other meat or shrimp for the pork, or just use mushrooms.

KAO SOI
Chiang Mai Noodles with Curry Sauce

> *Kao soi* is a signature dish of the city of Chiang Mai, and shops with a reputation for serving a commendable version stay extremely busy all day long. Made with either chicken or beef, the dish has Burmese origins, but has evolved into several versions with a clear Thai stamp. The curry sauce is mild with a salty-sour note, but it comes with a garnish of chilies fried in oil for those who like a fiery taste.

3/4 cup coconut cream
1 tablespoon Red Curry Paste (page 171)
1 teaspoon ground turmeric
1 pound chicken thighs, boned and cut into bite-sized chunks
4 cups coconut milk
3 tablespoons fish sauce
1 tablespoon soy sauce
1 tablespoon dark sweet soy sauce
1 teaspoon salt
2 tablespoons freshly squeezed lime juice
3 tablespoons vegetable oil
2 tablespoons coarsely ground dried red chili
1/2 cup pickled Chinese cabbage, such as Tientsin pickled vegetable
1/2 cup coarsely cut shallot
1 lime, cut lengthwise into 6 wedges
1 pound fresh Chinese-style egg noodles (bamee), *cooked until tender, well drained, rinsed in cold water, and drained again*
1/2 cup thinly sliced green onion (sliced crosswise)

In a large, heavy-bottomed saucepan, warm the coconut cream over medium heat until it boils gently. Adjust the heat to maintain a gentle boil and cook for 6 to 8 minutes, stirring occasionally. The coconut cream will become fragrant as it thickens. When you see tiny pools of oil glistening on the surface, add the curry paste and turmeric and stir to dissolve the paste into the coconut cream. Continue cooking for 1 to 2 minutes, until the curry paste has a pleasing aroma.

Add the chicken and stir-fry to coat it evenly with the paste. Cook for about 2 minutes. Increase the heat and add the coconut milk, fish sauce, both soy sauces, and salt; stir well. Adjust the heat to maintain a gentle, active boil and cook for 8 to 10 minutes, stirring occasionally. Remove from the heat, stir in the lime juice. Taste and adjust seasoning to your liking.

In a small skillet over low heat, warm the oil. Add the ground chili and fry for 3 or 4 minutes. Transfer the chili and oil to a small saucer. Place the saucer on a small serving platter along with the pickled cabbage, shallot, and lime in separate piles.

To serve, place a handful of cooked noodles in each large individual serving bowl. Ladle a serving of chicken and curry sauce into each bowl, add a sprinkling of green onion, and serve at once along with the garnishes.

SERVES 8 TO 10.

NOTE: *Kao soi* is traditionally garnished with a handful of cooked egg noodles fried into a crunchy nest. Deep-fry small nests of cooked noodles in deep, hot vegetable oil for 1 to 2 minutes. Drain on paper towels and set aside until serving time. Place a nest atop each bowl of curry noodles just before serving.

Egg noodles are always used with *kao soi,* both thin, flat ones similar to linguine and slender ones similar to spaghetti. Any type of cooked noodles will be delicious with this curry sauce.

KAO TAEN
Crispy Rice Cakes with Palm Sugar

This sweet snack, called *nahng let* in central Thailand, came to the north from Laos, but today it's popular all over the kingdom. Rice cakes are made by shaping warm, freshly steamed sticky rice into disks, drying them in the sun or in a warm oven, and then frying them crisp in hot oil. The dried rice cakes swell and bloom into puffy white blossoms, and are crowned with a delectable swirl of caramelized palm sugar.

You'll need to plan ahead for this dish. If you soak the rice overnight, and then steam it and shape the cakes the next morning, you can fry the *kao taen* in the afternoon or evening. The dried, unfried cakes, sealed airtight, will keep well for a month.

3 cups hot, cooked Sticky Rice (page 165)
Vegetable oil for deep-frying
1 cup palm sugar

Prepare the rice and spread the hot rice out on a large tray or baking sheet. Wet a wooden spoon and quickly and gently spread the rice into a shallow layer to release some of the steam and moisture. As soon as the rice cools enough to touch, shape it into small, thin disks, 2 or 3 inches in diameter and 3 or 4 grains thick. Make them as thin as you can, but resist the urge to press them into submission or they will be very hard. Work fast—the cakes needn't be perfectly round; a ragged edge is fine. Wet your fingers a little now and then if the rice sticks to your hands.

Place the shaped disks on cooling racks or trays to air-dry as you work. When all the disks are formed, set them in the full sun until brittle and very dry, turning them over several times to dry them evenly, 6 to 8 hours.

To fry the cakes, pour the oil into a wok or large, deep skillet to a depth of 3 inches. Place over medium heat and heat to 325° to 350°F. Meanwhile, line a platter or bowl with paper towels and place a large, long-handled mesh scoop or slotted spoon by the pan for turning the disks in the oil and for removing them as they are cooked.

Drop a small piece of rice cake into the pan. If it sinks to the bottom and then immediately floats to the top, blooms, and puffs, the oil is ready. Gently slide 3 cakes along the side of the pan into the oil and tend them as they float and swell into thick, white crackers. Turn them when they stop swelling on the first side, and let them cook on the other side just until they're fully puffed. Before they begin to brown, transfer them to the towel-lined platter to drain. Continue frying in batches of 3 cakes until all are cooked.

Place the palm sugar in a small, heavy-bottomed saucepan and bring to a gentle boil over medium heat. Simmer, stirring occasionally, until the sugar melts into a syrup and darkens to a rich caramel color somewhere between honey and maple syrup, 5 to 10 minutes. The sugar should form a shiny ribbon when it is dribbled from a spoon. Quickly drizzle some of the syrup onto each rice cake in a spiral design, starting at the center and twirling out to the edge. Let the rice cakes dry at room temperature until the sugar sets. They can be stored in an airtight container for up to 1 week.

MAKES 24 TO 36 RICE CAKES.

NOTE: If full sunshine isn't a practical option, dry the cakes in a warm oven (150°F) for about 3 hours. The oven will be faster than a sunbath, so check them every hour and remove them as soon as they're dry. They shouldn't brown at all. You could also leave them out on a counter to air dry for 1 or 2 days, turning them occasionally.

Thai cooks decorate *kao taen* by shaping a simple cone, with a small opening at the point, from a piece of banana leaf. The caramelized palm sugar is poured into the cone and allowed to drip out the opening onto the rice cakes.

KAO TAEN KEM
Crispy Rice Cakes with Garlic, Cilantro, and Pepper

For these delicious crispy rice cakes, freshly steamed sticky rice is seasoned with cilantro, garlic, and pepper and sun-dried in a large sheet. The sheet is then broken into pieces, which are fried crisp and eaten as a savory snack.

You will need to plan ahead to make these cakes because the rice must soak for at least 3 hours and must dry for 6 to 8 hours before it's ready to fry. If you soak the rice overnight, then steam it and dry it the next morning, you can cook a batch of the cakes in midafternoon. The dried, unfried rice cakes will keep for 1 month in a tightly sealed container, so you can cook them whenever you like.

3 cups hot, cooked Sticky Rice (page 165)
2 tablespoons vegetable oil, plus vegetable oil for deep-frying
2 tablespoons Cilantro Pesto (page 168)
1 tablespoon sugar
1 teaspoon salt

Prepare the rice and keep hot.

In a small skillet over medium heat, warm the 2 tablespoons of oil for 30 seconds. Add the pesto, sugar, and salt and stir-fry for 2 minutes. Remove from the heat.

Combine the pesto with the hot rice and mix it in slowly and carefully to season the rice well. Spread the seasoned rice out on a large tray or baking sheet. With your fingers, gently spread out the rice and pat it into a large, thin, fairly even sheet, 3 or 4 grains thick. Wet your fingers now and then if the rice sticks to your hands.

Put the sheet out in full sun until brittle and very dry, turning it after a few hours, for 6 to 8 hours. Break the sheet into 2- or 3-inch chunks.

To fry the chunks, pour the oil into a wok or large, deep skillet to a depth of 3 inches. Place over medium heat and heat to 325° to 350°F. Meanwhile, line a platter or bowl with paper towels and place a large, long-handled mesh scoop or slotted spoon by the pan for turning the cakes in the oil and for removing them as they are cooked.

Drop a small piece of rice cake into the pan. If it sinks to the bottom and then immediately floats to the top, blooms, and puffs, the oil is ready. Gently slide 3 or 4 chunks of the rice sheet along the sides of the pan into the oil and tend them as they float and swell into thick, pale crackers. Turn them when they stop swelling on the first side, and let them cook on the other side just until they're fully puffed. Before they begin to brown, transfer them to the towel-lined platter to drain. Continue frying in batches of 3 or 4 chunks until all the rice cakes are cooked.

Cool the cakes to room temperature and serve, or store in an airtight container for up to 1 week.

MAKES 24 TO 36 RICE CAKES.

NOTE: If full sunshine isn't a practical option, dry the rice sheet in a warm oven (150 °F) for about 3 hours. The oven will be faster than a sunbath, so check the sheet every hour and remove it as soon as it is dry. It shouldn't brown at all. You could also leave the sheet out on a counter to air-dry for 1 or 2 days, turning occasionally.

NAHM TAKRAI
Lemongrass Drink

Takrai means "lemongrass," and it's also the name of a restaurant in the charming northern Thai city of Chiang Mai. Takrai Restaurant grows its namesake herb in huge pots scattered throughout its alfresco dining room. Each day cooks trim off bouquets of the slender green leaves to make this simple, refreshing drink.

Even in Thailand it's difficult to buy lemongrass with its leaves attached, since stalks are trimmed to about ten inches in preparation for market. But you can make a pleasing version of *nahm takrai* using the sturdy top portion of the trimmed stalks, as long as they're fresh and soft green. The delicate flavor of this piquant drink fades quickly, so try to make it right before you want to serve it.

*A handful of fresh lemongrass leaves, preferably the soft grassy tops, or the top
half of 12 fresh green stalks*
3 cups cold water
1/4 cup Sugar Syrup (page 187)
Ice cubes

Cut the leaves or tops into 2-inch lengths; measure out 1 1/2 cups, loosely packed. In a blender jar, combine the tops, water, and syrup and blend at high speed until the water is a vivid green and the lemongrass leaves are reduced to fine, short, needlelike pieces, about 1 minute. Strain through a very fine sieve into a large bowl or pitcher; spoon off and discard the green foam.

Taste the drink to see if it's sweet enough, and add more syrup if you like. Serve in tall glasses over ice.

SERVES 4.

PAHK DAI
The South

Having spent my years in Thailand in the northeast and Bangkok, I was dazzled by the tropical splendor of the south. When I woke up on the overnight express train to Nakorn Srithammaraht, I saw what year-round rains and tropical heat can do. The south is green and lush, the horizon punctuated here and there with startling mountains, like isolated towers. They reminded me of the mountains in Chinese scroll paintings—craggy limestone monoliths that seem two-dimensional, like facades on a movie set. Pristine beaches lined with lissome coconut palms grace both coasts of the Malay peninsula, and rubber plantations and orchards cover the verdant rolling countryside in between.

The cuisine of southern Thailand is as distinctive as the landscape and as Pasah Dai, the unique dialect of the region. Southern Thais love *rote jaht,* or "intense, sharp flavor." First and foremost of the southern flavors is *rote peht*—the hot bursts of edible fire from fresh and dried chilies and peppercorns. But the puckery notes of lime and vinegar and the sweet-sour contrast of tamarind are much appreciated as well.

Southerners have a particular affection for sourness, so they enjoy an array of strong-flavored herbs and young leaves—*sadao, pahk gratin, pahk grachet*—that impart a sour, sometimes even bitter accent. They buy them, along with the tender new leaves of tamarind and cashew trees, in the market or pluck them from the source and enjoy them raw as part of a salad, mixed with noodles, or stirred into soups.

To mellow these fierce, dominant flavors, southerners delight in *rote faht-faht,* the cool taste of raw vegetables, particularly beans and sprouts. Familiar vegetables such as mung bean sprouts and raw green peas, fava beans, and green beans will help you understand *rote faht-faht,* although nothing is as memorable, either in appearance or taste, as the *sataw* bean. *Sataw* beans are a feature of southern cuisine so unusual and so beloved that they are an emblem of the culture in other regions of the kingdom. A southern Thai contingent within the Thai legislature is known as *luke sataw,* or "*sataw* beans."

An Indian influence, albeit subtle, permeates southern Thai food. *Kao moke gai*, a delicious chicken and rice dish, uses turmeric, a member of the ginger family prominent in Indian cooking. Turmeric has little flavor but is prized for the gorgeous carroty yellow color it bestows on savory dishes.

Gaeng mussamun, a southern curry that has long been a favorite all over the country, uses sweet Indian spices with abandon—cinnamon, cloves, nutmeg, mace, and cardamom—and includes an Indian flourish of potatoes and peanuts as well. It is made with beef or chicken, and has a rich, sweet tamarind note that sets it apart from all other Thai curries.

The kingdom's large Muslim population makes its home in southern Thailand. The three provinces closest to the Malaysian border are predominantly Islamic, with mosques in every town and village calling the faithful to prayer five times each day. Many people speak Malay and follow the dietary laws of Islam. These forbid the eating of pork and the consumption of alcohol and require that other meats for the table be slaughtered in accordance with traditional religious law.

Fish is eaten more than anything else in the south. *Gaeng leuang*, a hot curry of freshwater fish, is a classic dish similar to *gaeng som*, a clear, sour curry popular throughout the country. Despite the fact that the region is sandwiched between two seas, much of the fish southern Thais eat is freshwater. Seafood is a luxury, as it is throughout Thailand. With elegant Thai, Chinese, and European seafood restaurants eager to pay top dollar for the freshest catch, southern fishing boats send a great deal of their harvest racing toward Bangkok, and what remains in southern coastal markets commands a high price.

Southern Thai food is the least well known of any of Thailand's regional cuisines, perhaps because until transportation development within the last decade, the south was isolated from the rest of the kingdom. It's a paradise worth exploring, in person if you're blessed with the opportunity to travel to this tropical paradise, or else in your daydreams as you lazily toss your plate of *kao yum* or patiently turn your skewers of *satay*.

KAO YUM
Red-Hot Rice Salad

Kao yum is room-temperature jasmine rice tossed with an array of fresh herbs, vegetables, and fruit, and bound with a generous dash of dried ground chili and a rich, salty-sweet sauce. In southern Thai markets, speedy vendors toss a portion to your specifications, but on special occasions *kao yum* is a spectacular presentation, with the rainbow of ingredients beautifully presented to delight the eyes before pleasing the palate. The ingredient list is daunting, even for Thai cooks, but you can make a simplified version using the rice, the sauce, and whichever ingredients you can find in your market.

KAO YUM SAUCE
3 stalks fresh lemongrass
9 quarter-sized slices fresh galanga or ginger
9 fresh wild lime leaves or 2 tablespoons freshly grated lime zest
1 cup fish sauce
2 3/4 cups water
1 cup palm sugar or brown sugar

SALAD
6 cups cooked Jasmine Rice (page 164), at room temperature
1 cup shredded fresh coconut or dried coconut
1 cup dried shrimp, pounded to a coarse powder or finely chopped
1/4 cup coarsely ground dried chili
1 cup thinly sliced winged beans or green beans (sliced crosswise)
1 cup shelled sataw beans
1 small cucumber, thinly sliced and slices quartered (about 1 cup)
1 cup bean sprouts
1 cup finely diced, peeled pomelo, grapefruit, or orange meat
1 cup slivered, peeled green mango or unpeeled small apple chunks
2 stalks fresh lemongrass, trimmed and thinly sliced crosswise
*25 fresh wild lime leaves, sliced crosswise into very thin threads, or 2 tablespoons
  finely chopped fresh lime zest*

To make the sauce, trim the lemongrass stalks. Cut away and discard the grassy tops of each stalk, leaving a stalk about 6 inches long. Cut away any hard root section to leave a clean, smooth, flat base at the root end below the bulb. Remove and discard the tough outer leaves. Using the blunt edge of a cleaver or large knife, bruise each stalk, whacking it firmly at 2-inch intervals and rolling it over to bruise the stalk on all sides. Cut each stalk into 3-inch lengths and place the pieces in a medium-sized saucepan along with the galanga.

Tear the lime leaves in half and add them to the pot along

with the fish sauce, water, and palm sugar. Bring the mixture to a rolling boil over high heat. Reduce the heat to maintain a gentle boil and simmer until the sauce is dark and thickened, about 20 minutes. It should be as thick as real maple syrup and thinner than honey.

Remove from the heat and cool to room temperature. Strain, discarding the solids, and cover the sauce. Set aside at room temperature until ready to serve. The sauce will keep covered at room temperature for 1 or 2 days.

To prepare the salad, cook the rice and cool to room temperature. Meanwhile, in a small skillet over medium heat, dry-fry the coconut until lightly browned and fragrant, tossing frequently to brown evenly and avoid burning, 3 to 5 minutes. Set aside to cool.

Prepare all of the remaining salad ingredients and arrange them, along with the cooled coconut, in small separate piles on a large platter or in small separate bowls. Pour the cooled sauce into a small bowl as well. To serve, place 1 cup of the rice on each plate. First each diner sprinkles a serving of the rice with spoonfuls of as many of the accompaniments as desired. Then he or she drizzles 1 or 2 spoonfuls of the sauce over the rice and tosses to combine all of the ingredients into a fragrant, chaotic pile.

SERVES 6 TO 8.

NOTE: You can substitute a handful of dried galanga pieces for the fresh galanga in the sauce.

Whether you use pomelo, grapefruit, or orange, you will want only the pure, juicy meat from the sections and none of the stringy membranes.

Green mango adds a fruity, sour bite, but it's often difficult to find. If you substitute apple, try to find a sour one. Or use coarsely chopped, fresh pineapple instead, preferably one that isn't quite ripe.

To substitute frozen lima beans for shelled sataw beans, thaw and peel them, and don't worry if they split in half. Limas lack the peculiar taste of sataw beans, but they work beautifully as a substitute nonetheless. Peeled, shelled fresh fava beans also work well. Or sugar snap peas or snow peas may be used.

Kao yum calls for freshly made rice that has cooled to room temperature. Plan to make it the same day, preferably just a few hours before serving. Do not refrigerate the rice.

MOO SATAY
Grilled Pork on Skewers with Cucumber Salad and Spicy Peanut Sauce

Satay is skewers of meat marinated in coconut milk and spices and grilled quickly over charcoal. Originating in Indonesia, this tasty dish has traveled north up the peninsula to be adapted to suit local tastes by cooks in Malaysia and Thailand. It's street food, prepared by vendors with portable grills who set up shop near markets and popular restaurants. Waitresses will pass along your satay order to the vendor, fetch it, and obligingly figure the transaction into your total bill.

Thais use pork and a creamy peanut sauce for *satay*, while their predominantly Muslim neighbors to the south use beef. *Satay* is delicious and a favorite with guests, but it takes some time to prepare, so plan ahead and call for help on the skewering and grilling work.

MEAT
1/2 cup coconut milk
1 teaspoon fish sauce
1 teaspoon brown sugar
1/2 teaspoon ground cumin
1/2 teaspoon ground coriander
1/2 teaspoon ground turmeric
1 pound lean pork

SPICY PEANUT SAUCE
1/2 cup coconut milk
2 tablespoons Red Curry Paste (page 171)
1/2 cup chunky-style peanut butter
1/2 cup chicken stock
3 tablespoons palm sugar or brown sugar
2 tablespoons Tamarind Liquid (page 185) or freshly squeezed lime juice
1 tablespoon fish sauce
1/2 teaspoon salt

CUCUMBER PICKLES
1/2 cup white vinegar
1/2 cup water
1/2 cup sugar
1 teaspoon salt
6 small cucumbers or 1 large hothouse cucumber or Japanese cucumber
3 tablespoons coarsely chopped shallot or purple onion
1 teaspoon finely chopped fresh hot chili
1 tablespoon finely chopped dry-roasted peanuts
A few fresh cilantro leaves

To prepare the meat, combine coconut milk, fish sauce, sugar, cumin, coriander, and turmeric in a bowl and stir well. Slice the pork into long, thin strips, about 3 inches by 1 inch. Add the pork to the seasoned coconut milk, mix well, cover, and refrigerate for 1 to 2 hours. Immerse 60 small bamboo skewers in water to cover.

To prepare the sauce, warm the coconut milk in a small saucepan over medium heat. Stirring occasionally, heat the milk until it reaches a gentle boil and tiny beads of oil glisten on the surface, about 5 minutes. Add the curry paste and stir occasionally until it dissolves into the coconut milk and releases its fragrance, about 3 minutes. Add the peanut butter, chicken stock, and sugar and cook gently until the sauce is smooth, about 5 minutes. Remove from the heat and season with tamarind, fish sauce, and salt. Taste and adjust for a pleasing balance of sweet, sour, and salty. Cool to room temperature.

To prepare the pickle, combine the vinegar, water, sugar, and salt in a small saucepan over medium heat. Bring to a gentle boil, stirring to dissolve sugar and salt. Remove from the heat and cool to room temperature.

Just before serving time, peel the cucumbers, slice them crosswise about 1/4 inch thick, and cut the slices in half. Combine the cucumber slices with the vinegar dressing, shallot, and chilies and divide between 2 serving bowls. Sprinkle each serving with peanuts and garnish with a few leaves of cilantro.

Prepare a fire in a charcoal grill or preheat a gas grill or a broiler. Set out prepared peanut sauce and cucumber pickles and a serving platter for the grilled meat. Thread a slice of the marinated meat onto each soaked bamboo skewer and place alongside the grill.

Grill the skewered meat until cooked, turning as needed, 4 to 6 minutes total cooking time. Serve at once with peanut sauce and pickles.

SERVES 6 TO 8.

NOTE: You can use chicken, beef, or shrimp instead of pork, adjusting the grilling time as needed.

In Malaysia, *satay* comes with small, soft rice cakes, but in Thailand it's often served with toast points. Both are pleasing additions for enjoying the delicious sauce. Make the toast on the grill as you tend the skewered meat.

Thai cooks make their own coarsely ground unsalted peanut butter. To make your own, dry-fry raw peanuts or toast them in the oven until browned, then pound and grind them to a coarse paste in a mortar with a pestle.

This dish can be made in advance. For the meat, mix the marinade ingredients and refrigerate for up to 1 day. Combine the marinade with meat 1 or 2 hours before serving time. For the cucumber pickles, make the dressing and refrigerate for up to 1 day. Add the cucumbers, shallot, chili, and garnishes just before serving so everything will be crisp. For the *satay* sauce, make the sauce up to the point where you add the tamarind, fish sauce, and salt. Cover and refrigerate the cooled sauce for up to 1 day. At serving time, warm it very gently, add the seasonings, and serve warm or at room temperature.

NAHM PRIK JONE
Pirate-Style Chili Dipping Sauce with Fresh Vegetables

A red-hot southern specialty, this *nahm prik* is unusual in that the ingredients are left in chunks rather than pounded to a paste or smooth sauce. *Jone* means "pirate" or "bandit," and if outlaws invented this dish, I'm guessing they simply didn't have time to pound their sauces while escaping the long arm of the law.

Nahm prik jone is an example of *rote jaht,* the sharp, strong taste southerners enjoy. *Sataw* beans are traditional on the vegetable platter, and you may find them frozen in Thai markets. You can use fresh fava beans, sugar snap peas or snow peas, or frozen lima beans instead.

1/4 pound fresh shrimp, unpeeled
2 tablespoons shrimp paste
2 tablespoons fish sauce
2 tablespoons freshly squeezed lime juice
1 tablespoon Tamarind Liquid (page 185)
3 tablespoons water
2 tablespoons palm sugar or brown sugar
2 tablespoons thinly sliced fresh kii noo *chilies or finely chopped fresh serrano chilies*
2 tablespoons coarsely chopped, thinly sliced onion
2 tablespoons finely chopped dried shrimp
6 green beans, trimmed and halved crosswise
1/2 cup shelled sataw *beans*
1 wedge green cabbage (about 2 inches wide at widest point)
6 cherry tomatoes, halved lengthwise

Bring a medium saucepan filled with salted water to a rolling boil. Add the fresh shrimp and cook just until they turn pink and are opaque, about 2 minutes. Immediately immerse the shrimp in cool water, then peel, devein, coarsely chop, and set aside.

Wrap the shrimp paste in a small square of aluminum foil. Cook the packet in a dry small skillet over medium heat for about 5 minutes, turning once. Remove the packet from the heat and set aside to cool.

In a small bowl, combine the fish sauce, lime juice, tamarind, and water. Add the sugar and shrimp paste and stir, mashing and scraping to combine well. Add the chilies, onion, dried shrimp, and fresh shrimp and stir well. Taste and adjust seasoning to your liking.

Place the sauce in a small serving bowl on a platter. Arrange the vegetables around the dipping sauce and serve.

SERVES 4 TO 6.

NOTE: To substitute frozen lima beans for shelled *sataw* beans, thaw and peel them, and don't worry if they split in half. Limas lack the peculiar taste of *sataw* beans, but they work beautifully as a substitute nonetheless. Peeled, shelled fresh fava beans also work well.

KAO MOKE GAI
Chicken with Crispy Shallots in Yellow Rice

Kao moke gai means "chicken hidden in rice," an apt description of how this Indian-style dish is cooked. It is Thailand's version of the fabulous *biryanis* of northern India. As in India, the rice is salted before cooking, and some versions of *kao moke gai* include potatoes, fried golden and mixed with the rice.

1 teaspoon ground cayenne pepper
1 teaspoon ground cumin
1 teaspoon ground coriander
1/2 teaspoon ground turmeric
1/2 teaspoon freshly ground white pepper
2 1/2 teaspoons salt
6 chicken thighs (about 1 1/2 pounds)
2 tablespoons vegetable oil, plus vegetable oil for deep-frying shallots
5 quarter-sized slices fresh ginger
1 tablespoon coarsely chopped garlic
1/2 cup coarsely chopped yellow onion
2 cups jasmine rice or regular long-grain white rice
2 3/4 cups water
1/2 cup shallots, thinly sliced crosswise
1/2 cup white vinegar
1/4 cup sugar
3 fresh green serrano chilies, thinly sliced crosswise
4 small cucumbers, peeled and sliced on the diagonal into thin ovals
A handful of fresh cilantro leaves

In a small bowl, combine the cayenne, cumin, coriander, turmeric, white pepper, and 1/2 teaspoon of the salt. Mix together well. Sprinkle half of the spice mixture over the chicken pieces, rubbing in the spices to coat each piece well. Set aside both the coated chicken pieces and the remaining spice mixture.

In a large, flameproof casserole, heat the 2 tablespoons oil over moderately high heat. Add the chicken thighs, skin side down, and brown them well, turning as needed, 8 to 10 minutes. Remove the chicken pieces to a shallow bowl, cover, and set aside.

Pour off some of the oil, leaving about 2 tablespoons. Be careful not to discard any browned bits left from cooking the chicken. Reheat the oil remaining in the pan and add the ginger, turning and pressing it into the oil for about 30 seconds. Add the garlic and toss with a spatula until golden brown, 30 to 45 seconds.

Add the onion and the remaining spice mixture. Stir-fry until the onion is softened and translucent, about 1 minute. Add the rice and toss until the spiced oil coats and colors each grain.

Add the water and 1 1/2 teaspoons of the salt to the pan. Bring the rice to a vigorous boil over high heat, stirring occasionally to discourage grains from sticking to the bottom. Boil the rice until the surface becomes dry and the grains begin to swell, 5 to 7 minutes. Reduce the heat to low. Return the chicken pieces to the pan and, using a spatula or wooden spoon, bury them, one by one, near the bottom of the pan, under the partially cooked rice. Add any chicken juices that have collected in the bowl to the pan as well. Smooth out the rice to hide the chicken completely, cover, and cook over low heat until rice is tender and chicken is cooked through, about 30 minutes.

Meanwhile, in a wok or small skillet, pour in oil to a depth of 2 inches. Heat the oil over medium-high heat until hot but not smoking. Drop a piece of shallot into the pan. If it sizzles immediately, the oil is ready. Sprinkle the shallots over the surface of the oil, and, using a fork or a slotted spoon, separate and turn them quickly. As soon as most of the shallots are light brown, remove them with a slotted spoon to drain on paper towels until cool enough to touch. Then spread them out on a small plate and set aside, uncovered.

When the rice and chicken are done, remove the pan from the heat and let stand, covered, for about 15 minutes while you prepare the sauce and garnishes. In a small ceramic or glass mixing bowl, combine the vinegar, sugar, and the remaining 1/2 teaspoon of salt, stirring or whisking well until the sugar is completely dissolved and the liquid thickens slightly. Sprinkle the chili slices on top of the sauce and transfer this sweet-sour dressing to a small serving bowl.

To serve, dig the chicken pieces out of the rice, scraping away any clinging rice grains, and set them aside. Toss the rice with a fork to separate the grains, remove and discard the ginger slices, and mound the rice on a serving platter. Arrange the chicken on the platter with the rice, and garnish the dish with the cucumber slices, cilantro leaves, and crispy shallots. Serve warm or at room temperature with the sauce alongside.

SERVES 6.

HAW MOKE PHUKET
Fish in Yellow Curry Steamed in Banana Leaf Packets

Here is the southern Thai version of *haw moke*, which means "wrapped up and hidden." I had this at a waterside seafood restaurant on the breathtakingly beautiful resort island of Phuket. Southerners love the sunny color of turmeric and since seafood is plentiful, they use saltwater fish instead of the freshwater fish used in *haw moke* in the other regions of Thailand. You can wrap your packets in soft, fresh corn husks or parchment paper, or steam the thick curry mixture in a small shallow serving dish. If you don't have fresh wild lime leaves, use lime zest or add a handful of fresh herbs cut into thin strips.

9 small dried red chilies
2 stalks fresh lemongrass
2 tablespoons coarsely chopped garlic
2 tablespoons coarsely chopped shallot
1/2 teaspoon ground turmeric
1/2 teaspoon salt
9 whole black peppercorns
1/4 cup coconut cream
1/2 teaspoon sugar
1/2 pound sea bass, snapper, cod, or other saltwater fish fillet, cut crosswise
  into 1-inch pieces
Banana leaves for wrapping
9 fresh wild lime leaves, sliced crosswise in thin strips, or 2 tablespoons freshly
  grated lime zest
1 cup stemmed small spinach leaves

Stem the chilies and shake out and discard the seeds. Chop coarsely and place in a small bowl. Add warm water to cover and soak for 20 minutes.

Trim the lemongrass stalks. Cut away and discard the grassy tops, leaving a stalk about 3 inches long. Cut away any hard root sections to leave a clean, smooth, flat base at the root end below the bulb. Remove and discard tough outer leaves. Slice each stalk crosswise very thinly. Finely chop the slices.

Drain the chilies and place in a heavy mortar. Add the garlic, shallot, lemongrass, turmeric, salt, and peppercorns. With a pestle, pound and grind until a coarse paste forms, 5 to 10 minutes. Set aside.

In a small bowl, combine the curry paste with the coconut cream, sugar, and fish, and stir well. Let stand for 10 minutes. Meanwhile, cut the banana leaves into 4 rectangles each about 8 inches by 11 inches. Cut 4 additional rectangles about 3 inches by

6 inches. Place the large rectangles before you on a cutting board; place a smaller rectangle in the center of each. Stack several leaves of spinach on each small rectangle.

Stir the lime leaves into the fish curry, mixing well, and then divide the mixture evenly among the 4 sets of banana leaves, mounding it atop the spinach leaves. Fold the long edges of each large rectangle in to meet and overlap slightly in the center, forming a tube shape, and then carefully fold in the narrow ends to enclose the curry in the packet securely. Turn each packet over so that it is seam side down, and then tie the packets loosely with long, thin strips of banana leaf or thick cotton string.

Fill the bottom of a steamer pan or wok with water and bring to a rolling boil. Place the packets on a plate atop a steamer rack above the water. Cover the pan and begin timing. Cook over vigorously boiling water for 10 minutes.

Carefully transfer the packets to a serving platter and serve at once. Let each diner open his or her own packet.

SERVES 4.

GOONG PAHT SATAW
Shrimp Stir-Fried with Sataw Beans

The *sataw* bean, which grows in huge, ladderlike pods that droop down from trees in the forest, is beloved in southern Thailand although maligned in other regions. Some people say it has an unpleasant smell. I find it delicious, however, and not at all odiferous. In this simple stir-fry, shrimp is its perfect companion.

You can find frozen *sataw* beans in Thai markets. They resemble fava beans and lima beans, so either would make a good substitute. You also could even use fresh sugar snap peas or snow peas.

2 tablespoons vegetable oil
5 large garlic cloves, crushed
1/2 pound shrimp, peeled and deveined
1 1/2 cups shelled sataw *beans*
2 tablespoons fish sauce
2 teaspoons sugar

Heat a wok or large deep skillet over medium-high heat. Add the oil and swirl to coat the surface. When the oil is very hot, add the garlic and toss until lightly golden, about 15 seconds. Add the shrimp and toss for about 15 seconds. Add the *sataw* beans and toss again. Add the fish sauce and sugar, stir-fry another few seconds until the shrimp turns pink and the beans are tender.

Transfer onto a serving plate. Serve at once.

SERVES 4.

NOTE: To substitute frozen lima beans for shelled *sataw* beans, thaw and peel them, and don't worry if they split in half. Limas lack the peculiar taste of *sataw* beans, but they work beautifully as a substitute nonetheless. Peeled, shelled fresh fava beans also work well.

GAENG KAH-REE GAI
Kah-Ree Yellow Chicken Curry

This sunny-colored curry is a favorite both in Thailand and in the West. Chicken, potato, and onion are the classic combination, and shrimp is often substituted for chicken. Thais enjoy *kah-ree* curry with the same simple sweet-sour cucumber salad that accompanies *satay* (page 105).

3/4 cup coconut cream
3 tablespoons Yellow Curry Paste (page 173)
6 chicken thighs, boned and cut into bite-sized chunks
4 cups coconut milk
1/2 pound potatoes, peeled and cut into bite-sized chunks
1 large onion, cut lengthwise into thick wedges
2 tablespoons fish sauce
1 tablespoon palm sugar or brown sugar

In a medium, heavy-bottomed saucepan, warm the coconut cream over medium heat until it boils gently. Adjust the heat to maintain a gentle boil and cook for 6 to 8 minutes, stirring occasionally. The coconut cream will become fragrant as it thickens. When you see tiny pools of oil glistening on the surface, add the curry paste and stir to dissolve the paste into the coconut cream. Continue cooking for 3 to 4 minutes until the curry paste has a pleasing aroma.

Add the chicken and stir-fry for 1 to 2 minutes to coat it evenly with the paste. Cook for about 2 minutes. Increase the heat and add the coconut milk, potatoes, fish sauce, and sugar; stir well. Adjust the heat to maintain a gentle, active boil and cook for 6 to 8 minutes, stirring occasionally. Taste and adjust the seasoning with a little more fish sauce or sugar if needed.

Add the onion and cook until the chicken and potatoes are tender, about 5 minutes. Transfer to a serving bowl and serve hot or warm.

SERVES 6 TO 8.

NOTE: I prefer curries made with dark meat, particularly thighs or wings, but use whatever chicken parts you like, with or without skin.

To substitute shrimp for the chicken, add 1 pound shrimp, peeled and deveined, at the end, so that they cook only about 2 minutes. Or to make a vegetarian curry, stir-fry carrot or winter squash chunks with the paste, add mushrooms with the onion, and stir in snow peas and halved cherry tomatoes just before removing the curry from the heat.

To prepare the curry in advance, cook it only up to the point where the onion is added. Cool to room temperature, cover, and refrigerate for up to 24 hours. To serve, bring the curry back to a gentle boil over medium heat. Add the onion and continue as directed.

GAENG MUSSAMUN
Mussamun Curry with Beef, Potatoes, and Peanuts

> *Gaeng mussamun* is a special-occasion curry often served at wedding feasts. The sweet-spicy flavors of cinnamon, cloves, cardamom, mace, and nutmeg predominate over a background of dried red chilies. Along with these sweet spices, the inclusion of potatoes, peanuts, and tamarind reveal this curry's Indian origins. In Thailand, *mussamun* curries are traditionally made with chunks of beef, but chicken is popular as well. Advance preparation gives this curry's rich, delicious flavors time to develop.

5 cups coconut milk
2 pounds boneless beef, cut into 2-inch chunks
1 cup coconut cream
1/3 cup Mussamun Curry Paste (page 175)
3 tablespoons fish sauce
2 tablespoons palm sugar or brown sugar
3 tablespoons Tamarind Liquid (page 185)
12 whole cardamom pods
6 cinnamon sticks
2 pounds potatoes, peeled and cut into 2-inch chunks
1 large onion, cut lengthwise into thick wedges
1/2 cup dry-roasted peanuts
About 2 tablespoons freshly squeezed lime juice

In a large saucepan, bring the coconut milk to a gentle boil over medium heat. Add the beef chunks and simmer until the beef is tender, about 1 hour.

In a small, heavy-bottomed skillet over medium heat, bring the coconut cream to a gentle boil. Adjust the heat to maintain a gentle boil and cook for 6 to 8 minutes, stirring occasionally. The coconut cream will become fragrant as it thickens. When you see tiny pools of oil glistening on the surface, add the curry paste and stir to dissolve the paste in the coconut cream. Continue cooking for 3 to 4 minutes, until the curry paste has a pleasing aroma.

Scrape the curry paste into the pot with the beef and coconut milk; stir well. Add the fish sauce, sugar, tamarind, cardamom, cinnamon, and potatoes. Simmer for 10 minutes. Add the onions and peanuts and simmer until the potatoes are cooked, about 5 minutes. Taste and adjust seasoning until you have a pleasing sweet, sour, and salty balance. Add a little lime juice to sharpen the taste.

Serve warm.

SERVES 10.

NOTE: To substitute chicken for the beef, use 3 pounds chicken thighs, boned and cut into bite-sized chunks. Omit the initial long simmering in coconut milk called for with beef. Begin by cooking the curry paste in coconut cream over medium heat as directed. Stir in the chicken and cook it in the coconut-curry sauce until coated and browned, 3 to 5 minutes. Transfer the mixture to a large saucepan, add the coconut milk, and bring to a gentle boil over medium heat. Continue as directed in the beef recipe.

To prepare the curry in advance, cook it only up to the point where the onions are added. Cool to room temperature, cover, and refrigerate for up to 24 hours. To serve, bring the curry back to a gentle boil over medium heat. Add the onion and continue as directed.

GAENG LEUANG PAHK DAI
Sour Yellow Curry of Fish and Bamboo

A *gaeng* can be a soup or a curry, and this dish is a combination of the two. It uses a curry paste, but it's made with water instead of coconut milk, and sharpened with the sour notes of tamarind and lime. *Leuang* means "yellow"; turmeric and yellow chilies, called *prik leuang,* give a jolt of southern Thai color to the dish. These yellow chilies are very difficult to find, even in Thailand, but serrano or any other fresh hot chili works fine. The curry paste is quite similar to *gaeng som,* a clear, sour curry popular all over Thailand, so try it with purchased *gaeng som* curry paste and 1/2 teaspoon ground turmeric if you want to save time.

12 small dried red chilis
2 teaspoons salt
1 tablespoon coarsely chopped fresh yellow or serrano chili
3 heaping tablespoons finely chopped yellow onion
3 heaping tablespoons finely chopped garlic
1 teaspoon chopped, peeled fresh turmeric or ground turmeric
1 tablespoon shrimp paste
3 cups water
1 cup sliced canned bamboo shoots, rinsed under cold water and well drained
12 green beans, trimmed and halved crosswise
1/2 small pineapple, peeled, cored, and cut into thin, bite-sized chunks (about 1 cup)
2 tablespoons fish sauce
2 tablespoons Tamarind Liquid (page 185)
1 tablespoon palm sugar or brown sugar
1 pound meaty white fish fillet, such as catfish, snapper, sea bass, or cod, cut crosswise into 1-inch-wide pieces
1 to 2 tablespoons freshly squeezed lime juice

Stem the chilies and shake out and discard some of the seeds. Place in a small bowl, add warm water to cover, and soak for 15 minutes. Drain the chilies, chop coarsely, and place in a heavy mortar. Add the salt and pound and grind with a pestle until the chilies are broken down, 3 to 5 minutes. Add the fresh chili, onion, garlic, turmeric, and shrimp paste. Continue grinding and pounding, scraping down the sides with a spoon now and then, until you have a coarse paste, about 15 minutes. Set aside.

Bring the water to a boil in a large saucepan over medium heat. Stir in the curry paste, bamboo shoots, and green beans and cook for 5 minutes. Add the pineapple, fish sauce, tamarind, and sugar and cook for 3 minutes. Add the fish fillet and cook until done, 3 to 5 minutes. Remove from the heat and add the lime juice. Taste and adjust the seasoning to your liking; the flavor should be sharp and spicy. Serve hot or warm.

SERVES 6.

NOTE: Fresh yellow chilies are a gorgeous golden-orange color. As I pointed out in the introduction, they are very difficult to find in the West, and any fresh hot chili will do. Sometimes *kii noo* chilies ripen to an orange or red color, so these would be an especially good substitute; but don't worry—the turmeric you'll add is what gives the curry most of its trademark color.

This dish is traditionally made with a sour, pickled form of bamboo called *naw mai dong,* along with bamboo shoots and other vegetables such as green papaya and squash. Look for pickled bamboo in Asian markets if you'd like to try it. You can substitute other vegetables such as kabocha pumpkin, acorn squash, yellow squash, or zucchini, adjusting the cooking time as needed.

PAHK ISSAHN
The Northeast

Northeastern Thai food is a rustic, robust cuisine of grilled meats and incendiary sauces eaten with Laotian-style sticky rice. More than any of the other regional cuisines of Thailand, it is well known and wildly popular throughout the kingdom. Northeastern vendors can be found down every Bangkok alleyway, grilling garlicky chicken for *gai yahng* and pounding green papaya and chilies into *som tum*. Large open-air restaurants, called *suan ahahn,* or "food gardens," draw crowds of aficionados for the same culinary treats in an upscale setting.

In Thai, this northeastern region is translated as an unwieldy mouthful: *pahk tahwahn oke chin neua* (meaning roughly Northeast). But that's no problem, since the area is universally known as Pahk Issahn. It's the largest of Thailand's regions, covering more than one third of the country. The Mekong River meanders along its northernmost limits, forming the border with Laos, and the Dangkrek Mountains separate the southern portion of Issahn from Cambodia. The Laotian heritage of the majority of Issahn's people is evident in the cuisine, which is as similar to Laotian cooking as to be almost indistinguishable from it.

Between Laos and Cambodia lies the immense, flat plain of Issahn, which is home to millions of Thais. Most of them are rice farmers, but Issahn's notorious droughts often make farming impossible and send northeasterners to seek work in Bangkok.

During the dry season, the earth cracks and peels and everything turns brown under the ferocious sun. When the monsoon rains come, the change is dramatic. Voluptuous charcoal- and ash-colored clouds gather, muscling the dethroned sun out of the picture, and burst, often at around four in the afternoon. Despite the torrents of rain, and even with its complete predictability, umbrellas and raincoats aren't in evidence—it's just too wet. If you're caught somewhere, it's best to surrender and enjoy waiting out the downpour with a plate of *som tum*.

Issahn food is a triumph of ingenuity on the part of cooks who have little going for them in terms of climate, money, and raw materials.

The soil is anything but cooperative in putting forth crops, but *pahk boong*, the wild watercress that pokes out of the shallows by the river, does nicely as a salad or stir-fry. The nearest bamboo grove is a mine of fresh bamboo shoots, to be dug up, boiled to tenderness, and then pickled, stir-fried with chilies, or shredded for *soop naw mai*, a tasty bamboo salad with chilies, lime, and mint.

Economic problems may leave little money for buying meat in the market, but the rivers are alive with tasty fish, and all it takes is a net or a woven bamboo trap to catch dinner without spending a single *baht*. Catfish can become *tome yum plah dook*, the simple Issahn version of Thailand's famous hot-and-sour lemongrass soup. *Plah chone*, a large meaty fish, is marinated and grilled whole, or stuffed with lemongrass and cilantro, wrapped in banana leaves, and roasted in glowing coals. A resident flock of ducks and chickens can keep a family supplied with eggs for *kai kem* (salted eggs) and *kai jiow* (omelets), while providing a delicious curry on special occasions when a distinguished guest comes to call. Many an Issahn family has survived a hard season entirely on rice fortified with crushed dried red chilies and *plah rah*, a homemade fermented fish sauce.

Northeasterners love meat, and when times are good they turn ordinary cuts into rustic dishes that have given Issahn food its good name. Beef is grilled for *seua rong hai*, or salted, sun-dried, and fried crisp for *neua kem*. Both dishes have the kind of dipping sauces that give Issahn food a reputation for generating fireworks. Leftover grilled beef becomes *yum neua yahng nahm toke*, a searing salad with fresh mint, green onions, and lime to help quench the chili fire. *Lahp* is a similar salad, but it's made with minced pork or beef, and in one version, *lahp dip*, the meat is raw. Both these hearty salads contain *kao kua*, the roasted rice powder that is an Issahn trademark. Raw sticky rice is dry-fried until wheaty brown and aromatic, then pounded in a heavy mortar to a fine sandy state. It is an ingredient in many salads, adding a roasted flavor and a pleasing crunch.

If you're ready to explore the strong, inviting flavors of Issahn cooking, put your sticky rice in water to soak for a few hours, start the meat marinating, and sit down to shred a green papaya while you daydream your way to Pahk Issahn. The sun is glaring but you don't mind, since your friends are shading you with their parasols and offering you sweet iced coffee bouncing in a plastic bag bound with a rubber band. The air is an appetizing perfume of roasting chicken and juicy beef, and the sound of mortars and pestles pounding up hot savory sauces keeps time with the wail of *plaeng look toong*, the popular songs of the region that share the subject matter and spirit of country music in Nashville, U.S.A. It is *Boon Bahng Fai*, the rambunctious rocket festival designed to call the rains down for a good rice harvest. You'll need to find a shady spot from which to view the folk dancing, Thai boxing, and rocket launching while eating sticky rice and the vibrantly flavored dishes of the Issahn kitchen.

GAI YAHNG
Grilled Chicken

Gai yahng is northeastern street food, and a specialty so delicious that
it's become available throughout the kingdom. With green papaya salad
and sticky rice, garlicky grilled chicken is the quintessential Issahn meal.

1/3 cup Cilantro Pesto (page 168)
2 tablespoons soy sauce
1 teaspoon salt
1 chicken (about 4 pounds), cut into serving pieces
Sweet-Hot Garlic Sauce (page 189)

In a deep mixing bowl just large enough to hold the chicken,
combine the pesto, soy sauce, and salt. Add the chicken and turn
to coat well with the marinade. Cover and chill for 1 to 2 hours,
turning occasionally to season each piece well.

Prepare the Sweet-Hot Garlic Sauce and set aside.

Prepare a very hot fire in a charcoal grill or preheat a gas grill.
Arrange the chicken on the grill and cook 45 minutes to 1 hour,
turning occasionally to brown and cook evenly. When the chicken
is done, transfer it to a serving platter and serve hot, warm, or at
room temperature with the sauce.

SERVES 4 TO 6.

NOTE: Thais grill small free-range chickens, which they splay whole on
bamboo splints and hack into large pieces before serving. I like to make
gai yahng with halved Cornish hens or chicken wings.

SOM TUM
Green Papaya Salad with Chilies and Lime

This northeastern signature salad is wildly popular all over Thailand. It's a tangle of pale green shreds of unripe papaya infused with an incendiary combination of flavors. *Tum* means "to pound with a mortar and pestle." *Som* means "sour," and that's the dominant note in a chorus of chilies, fish sauce, garlic, and lime. While green papaya has little flavor, it provides a perfect crunchy foundation for this unique salad.

6 *fresh* kii noo *chilies, left whole, or 2 fresh serrano chilies, thinly sliced*
1 *tablespoon coarsely chopped garlic*
1 *teaspoon coarsely chopped shallot*
1 *small hard, green, unripe papaya, peeled and finely shredded (about 2 cups), or*
 1 *cup each finely shredded cabbage and carrot*
9 *green beans, trimmed and cut into 2-inch lengths*
1 *teaspoon palm sugar or sugar*
1/4 *teaspoon salt*
2 *tablespoons fish sauce*
1/2 *lime, quartered lengthwise*
7 *cherry tomatoes, quartered lengthwise*

In the bowl of a large, heavy mortar, combine the chilies, garlic, and shallot. Grind and pound with a pestle until they are broken down, but not completely mushy. Use a spoon to scrape down the sides now and then and mix everything in well.

Add the papaya and pound until the stiff shreds become limp and soft, about 3 minutes. Use the spoon to scrape and turn the mixture over as you work.

Add the green beans and pound to bruise them. One at a time, add the sugar, salt, and fish sauce, pounding a little after each addition. Squeeze in the juice from each piece of lime, then add the lime pieces to the mortar as well. Add the tomatoes and pound another minute, turning as before as the tomatoes release some of their liquid. Pound more gently so the liquid won't splash.

Taste the sauce in the bottom of the mortar and adjust the seasonings, which should be an interesting balance of sour, hot, salty, and sweet. Using a slotted spoon, transfer the salad to a small serving platter. Drizzle on some of the sauce remaining in the mortar and serve.

SERVES 4.

LAHP
Good Luck Salad

Lahp means "good fortune" and that auspicious name makes this hot and spicy meat dish a popular choice for Thai weddings and other celebrations. Made with coarsely chopped pork, beef, or chicken, it is also typical of the highly seasoned dishes called *gahp glaem,* or "drinking food," so-called because they go so well with beer and Thai whiskey.

1 cup chicken stock
1/2 pound coarsely ground pork, beef, or chicken
1/2 cup coarsely chopped shallot
3 tablespoons finely chopped green onion
2 tablespoons coarsely chopped fresh cilantro
A handful of fresh mint leaves
3 tablespoons freshly squeezed lime juice
2 tablespoons fish sauce
2 tablespoons Roasted Rice Powder (page 167)
1 tablespoon coarsely ground dried red chili
1/2 teaspoon sugar
A few lettuce leaves
2 wedges green cabbage (about 2 inches wide at the widest point)
6 green beans, trimmed and halved crosswise

In a small saucepan over high heat, bring the stock to a boil. Add the pork and cook for 1 to 2 minutes, tossing often with a large spoon to break up the meat and cook it through fairly evenly. When the meat is cooked, remove the pan from the heat.

Using a slotted spoon, transfer the meat to a medium bowl, leaving most of the liquid behind. Stir in the shallot, green onion, cilantro, and most of the mint, reserving a few leaves for a garnish. Add the lime juice, fish sauce, rice powder, chili, and sugar; stir to combine everything well. Taste and adjust seasoning as needed for a pleasing balance of sour, salty, and hot.

Line a serving platter with lettuce leaves and mound meat mixture in the center. Garnish with the cabbage, green beans, and the reserved mint. Serve at once.

SERVES 4.

NOTE: *Lahp* has more flavor if it is made with coarsely ground meat. Ask a butcher for coarse grind or chili grind, or cut the meat into large chunks and then chop it with a Chinese cleaver.

SEUA RONG HAI
Grilled Beef

The literal translation of this recipe's whimsical Thai name is "as the tiger weeps." The dish is thus called because it's made with fatty beef that drips oily "tears" onto fiery coals as it cooks. It's also called *neua yahng nahm toke,* or "beef grilled till the juices fall," and by either name, it's eaten with a feisty hot dipping sauce and sticky rice. Since *seua rong hai* marinates only an hour and cooks quickly, it's a perfect starter for a meal cooked on the grill.

1/4 cup soy sauce
1 tablespoon fish sauce
2 teaspoons sugar
1 pound beef rib-eye (with some fat) or lean flank steak
Dipping Sauce for Grilled Beef (page 191)

Combine the soy sauce, fish sauce, and sugar in a glass or ceramic bowl, stirring to dissolve the sugar. Add the beef and marinate for about 1 hour, turning occasionally. Meanwhile, prepare the dipping sauce and set aside.

Prepare a very hot fire in a charcoal grill or preheat a gas grill. The coals should be white-hot before you put the meat on and the grill rack should be several inches above the glowing coals, so that the meat will cook slowly enough to remain juicy and not burn. Place the meat on the rack and cook, turning occasionally, until it is pink at the center but dark and moist outside, 5 to 10 minutes. As the meat cooks, fat should drip onto the coals and flare up now and then.

When the meat is ready, transfer it to a serving platter. Slice the meat crosswise into thin slices and transfer the meat and its juices to a plate. Serve hot or warm with the dipping sauce.

SERVES 4.

NOTE: You can cook the meat for this dish under a preheated broiler or on a stove-top grill pan.

Since leftover Grilled Beef is the basic ingredient in Fiery Grilled Beef Salad (page 129), I always double this recipe while I've got the broiler or grill hot and enjoy the extra portion in the salad recipe the next day.

NEUA KEM/NEUA DAET DIOW
Salty Sun-Dried Beef

This solar-powered northeastern specialty has two names in Thai. *Neua kem* simply means "salty beef." *Daet diow* means "one day's sunshine," and that's what it takes to prepare this dish—a day in the sun dries the beef into leathery strips, ready to be fried and enjoyed with a robust dipping sauce made of roasted tomatoes, chilies, and garlic. Serve the beef with a great mound of sticky rice.

1/4 cup fish sauce
1 tablespoon sugar
1/2 teaspoon salt
1/2 teaspoon freshly ground pepper
1 pound flank steak
Roasted Tomato, Garlic, and Chili Sauce (page 192)
Vegetable oil for deep-frying
3 wedges green cabbage (about 2 inches wide at widest point)
3 leaves lettuce
3 small cucumbers, peeled and sliced on the diagonal into thick ovals

In a medium bowl, combine the fish sauce, sugar, salt, and pepper and stir until the sugar is dissolved. Set aside.

Using a sharp knife, slice the beef in half horizontally, cutting with the grain to make two large sheets. Cut halved pieces into long strips about 2 inches by 1 inch. Toss the beef in the fish sauce mixture to coat evenly. Marinate at room temperature for 1 to 2 hours.

Arrange the meat strips in a single layer on large trays and dry in the bright sunshine for 6 to 8 hours, or in a 200°F oven for 4 hours. Turn the meat occasionally as it darkens and dries.

Prepare the sauce and set aside in a small bowl.

Pour the oil into a wok or large, deep skillet to a depth of about 3 inches. Heat the oil until very hot, about 350° to 375°F. Working with small batches, fry the beef until crispy and brown but still moist inside, 2 to 3 minutes. Remove with a slotted spoon and drain well on paper towels. Transfer to a serving platter with cabbage, lettuce, cucumbers, and the bowl of sauce. Serve hot, warm, or at room temperature.

SERVES 6.

NOTE: Once it is salted and dried, the beef can be stored in an airtight container at room temperature for a few days.

YUM NEUA YAHNG NAHM TOKE
Fiery Grilled Beef Salad

A *yum* is a hearty salad of meat or seafood in a bracing, chili-lime dressing laced with fresh herbs. They are served at room temperature and, unlike most savory Thai dishes, they are not eaten with rice. This *yum* includes the crunch of roasted rice powder, a northeastern trademark added for its texture and fragrance.

Grilled Beef (page 127)
1/3 cup chicken stock
2 green onions, coarsely chopped, including some green tops
1/4 cup finely chopped shallot
A handful of fresh cilantro leaves, coarsely chopped
1 tablespoon Roasted Rice Powder (page 167)
1 teaspoon coarsely ground dried red chili
1 teaspoon sugar
1/4 cup fish sauce
1/4 cup freshly squeezed lime juice
3 leaves leaf lettuce
2 small cucumbers, peeled and sliced crosswise on the diagonal into thin ovals
5 cherry tomatoes, halved lengthwise
A handful of fresh mint sprigs

Thinly slice the cooked beef crosswise into 2-inch strips and set aside. In a small saucepan, bring the chicken stock to a gentle boil over medium heat. Add the beef and warm it in the stock for 1 minute, turning occasionally. Remove the pan from the heat and set aside.

Add the green onions, shallot, cilantro, rice powder, chili, sugar, fish sauce, and lime juice to the beef. Toss well. Taste the dressing and adjust it to your liking with additional fish sauce, lime juice, sugar, or chilies.

Arrange the lettuce leaves on a serving platter. With a slotted spoon, transfer the beef to the platter, mounding it on the lettuce. Drizzle the beef with some additional sauce from the pan and garnish with the cucumber, tomatoes, and mint. Serve as soon as possible, warm or at room temperature.

SERVES 4.

NOTE: Thais make this dish with fatty cuts of beef cooked quite rare, but you can use a lean cut cooked to your liking.

Rice powder is a traditional addition to this salad, but it is delicious without it. You can also omit the mint, if it's difficult to find.

SOOP NAW MAI
Shredded Bamboo Salad with Chilies, Lime, and Mint

The hot, sharp flavors of this rustic salad will sound reveille to your palate. It's perfect with sticky rice and an Issahn-style grilled meat such as Grilled Chicken (page 124) or Grilled Beef (page 127).

1 can (14 ounces) whole bamboo shoots, drained, rinsed, and drained again
2 tablespoons finely minced shallot
1 tablespoon finely minced garlic
2 tablespoons finely minced green onion
2 tablespoons fish sauce
1 tablespoon freshly squeezed lime juice
1 tablespoon Roasted Rice Powder (page 167)
1 teaspoon sugar
1 teaspoon coarsely ground dried red chili
A handful of fresh mint leaves
2 wedges green cabbage (about 2 inches wide at widest point)
9 green beans, trimmed and halved crosswise

Shred or cut bamboo shoots lengthwise into very thin strips about 2 inches long. Place in a mixing bowl. Add the shallot, garlic, and green onion and toss to combine. Add the fish sauce, lime juice, rice powder, sugar, and chili; toss well. Taste the sauce and adjust the seasoning until you have a pleasing balance of salty, sour, and hot. Reserving a few leaves for garnish, add the mint and toss well.

With a slotted spoon, transfer the salad to a serving platter. Spoon on a little of the sauce remaining in the bowl. Garnish the platter with the cabbage wedges and beans, arranging them in a pile alongside the bamboo shoot mixture. Serve at room temperature.

SERVES 4.

NOTE: For this salad, you'll need whole bamboo shoot tips. To shred them, halve the shoots lengthwise, thinly slice the halves lengthwise, and then cut into long, thin strips. You need a pale yellow tangle; the shreds do not need to be uniform in size.

PLAH PAO UBON
Grilled Whole Fish with Lemongrass and Graprao Basil

I enjoyed this dish at a picnic hosted by Vichai Viboonkijtanakor and his family in Ubon Raachatanii, a large town near the Laotian border famed for its celebrations of Wahn Khao Pahnsah, the beginning of the Buddhist lent. Vichai grilled our fish in the traditional way, on a bed of dry, fibrous coconut husks. He lit the coconut husks and let them burn slowly so that the fish cooked very gently. When the fire died, the fish was done. Cooks in the northeast grill large freshwater fish this way, but it works well with boneless whole trout or with fillets of any meaty fish.

Chili-Garlic Sauce (page 190)
1/4 cup fish sauce
2 tablespoons soy sauce
2 tablespoons finely minced garlic
1 teaspoon freshly ground pepper
1 teaspoon sugar
Banana leaves and aluminum foil for wrapping
3 stalks fresh lemongrass
2 bunches graprao basil or other fresh basil (about 1 1/2 cups leaves)
6 boneless small trout or 3 pounds meaty fish fillet, divided into 6 equal portions

Prepare a fire in a charcoal grill or preheat a gas grill. Prepare the Chili-Garlic Sauce and set aside.

In a small bowl, combine the fish sauce, soy sauce, garlic, pepper, and sugar. Stir well and set aside. Prepare six 8-by-14-inch sheets of aluminum foil and six 8-by-11-inch pieces of banana leaf. Place the 6 aluminum foil sheets on a flat work surface in front of you. Arrange 1 banana leaf piece in the center of each piece of aluminum foil.

Trim the lemongrass stalks. Cut away and discard the grassy tops of each stalk, leaving a stalk about 6 inches long. Cut away any hard root section to leave a clean, smooth, flat base at the root end below the bulb. Remove and discard tough outer leaves. Using the blunt edge of a cleaver or large knife, whack the stalk firmly at 2-inch intervals, rolling it over to bruise it on all sides. Slice each stalk on the diagonal into 2-inch lengths and set aside.

Place a whole fish or fish fillet on each banana leaf. Divide the fish sauce mixture among them, spooning it evenly over the fish to cover completely. Tuck several chunks of lemongrass and sprigs of basil inside each whole fish or alongside the fillets. Fold the long edges of each banana leaf toward the center and tuck in to enclose the fish securely. Fold all sides of the foil in toward the center to make a well-sealed packet.

Arrange the pockets on the grill rack and grill over hot coals for 8 to 10 minutes on each side. Transfer the packets to plates and serve at once with the Chili-Garlic Sauce.

SERVES 6.

NOTE: To prepare this dish in the traditional way, buy a 2- to 3-pound whole fish and have it cleaned and slit open from head to tail, leaving the bones intact. (Asian markets usually have excellent fresh fish and the staff to prepare them this way.) Rub the fish sauce mixture in the fish and then stuff it with the lemongrass and basil. Wrap in banana leaf and aluminum foil and grill for 15 to 20 minutes on each side.

If you can't easily find fresh Asian herbs, use the freshly grated zest of 3 limes or lemons instead of lemongrass, and cilantro, dill, mint, or any other fresh herb instead of the basil.

Like most Thai sauces, the chili sauce is served on the side, so you can add a plate of lime wedges or a quick sauce of lemon and melted butter for those who prefer a milder taste. The banana leaves enclosing the fish are wrapped in foil for grilling, so you can omit them if they're difficult to find.

OOH PLAH
Red Curry Catfish with Fresh Basil Steamed in Banana Leaves

Here is an Issahn-style version of the typical Thai dish called *haw moke*. A simple red curry paste is mixed with chunks of freshwater fish and aromatic herbs, wrapped in charming banana leaf packets, and briefly steamed. When you open the little green parcel, a lovely curry-herb aroma rises to greet you, inviting you to enjoy the delicious contents.

In Thailand, the banana leaves are wrapped into beautiful, tiny pyramids, but it takes very fresh, sturdy banana leaves and lots of practice under the discerning eye of an experienced Thai cook to master the skill. A simple folded packet works just as well.

Banana leaves are often available frozen in Asian markets, but you can also use fresh corn husks, or the dried ones found in Hispanic markets, which can be soaked to soften, just as they are for wrapping tamales. This dish can even be steamed in small saucers instead of leaves. In landlocked northeastern Thailand, *ooh plah* is always made with freshwater fish, but any firm-fleshed fish fillet will do.

10 small dried red chilies
1/2 teaspoon salt
2 tablespoons coarsely chopped garlic
1 tablespoon coarsely chopped shallot
1 tablespoon finely chopped, peeled fresh galanga or fresh ginger
1 tablespoon thinly sliced fresh lemongrass (sliced crosswise), finely chopped
2 teaspoons shrimp paste
1 pound catfish or other firm-fleshed fish fillet
1 tablespoon fish sauce
2 handfuls of fresh maengluk *basil leaves or other fresh basil leaves*
Banana leaves or soft, fresh corn husks

Stem the chilies and shake out most of the seeds. Coarsely chop the chilies and place in a small bowl. Add warm water to cover and soak for 20 minutes. Drain the chilies and place in a large, heavy mortar. Add the salt and pound and grind with a pestle until the chilies are broken down, 3 to 5 minutes. Take care not to splash incendiary chili goo in your eyes as you work. Add the garlic, shallot, galanga, lemongrass, and shrimp paste and continue grinding and pounding, scraping down the sides with a spoon now and then, until you have a coarse paste, about 5 minutes. Set aside.

Cut the fish fillets into large chunks, 2 inches by 1 inch. In a small bowl, combine the fish, curry paste, fish sauce, and 1 handful of the basil leaves. Set aside.

Cut the banana leaves into 12 rectangles, 6 inches by 8 inches. Set 6 of the rectangles on a flat working surface in front of you.

Place the other 6 rectangles squarely on top of them. Place a small pile of basil in the center of each pair of leaves, and cover it with a handful of the fish mixture. Fold the long edges of the rectangles in to meet in the center, and then carefully fold in the narrow ends to enclose the fish securely. Turn each packet over so that is is seam side down, and then tie the packets loosely with long, thin strips of banana leaf or thick cotton string.

Fill the bottom of a steamer pan or wok with water and bring to a rolling boil. Place the packets on a plate atop a steamer rack above the water. Cover the pan and begin timing. Cook over vigorously boiling water for 15 minutes. Carefully remove the packets from the steam and let stand for 10 to 15 minutes.

Serve warm or at room temperature.

SERVES 6.

NOTE: You can grind ingredients for the curry paste in a blender or small food processor if you prefer. Use a little of the chili water as needed to ease the blending. Or you can substitute 2 to 3 tablespoons prepared red curry paste.

Use a mixture of fresh cilantro leaves, chopped green onions, and a squeeze of lime juice if fresh basil is difficult to find.

GAENG BAH
Country-Style Curry

This is hearty, rustic fare, with a red-hot chili bite. Made with beef or pork and an array of fresh vegetables, it makes a tasty one-dish accompaniment to a generous helping of jasmine rice. *Gaeng bah* is usually made with the hard, golfball-sized Thai eggplants called *makeua poh,* but any eggplant will do. It's also wonderful with summer squash, baby corn, sugar snap peas, or snow peas. Adjust the cooking time according to the vegetables you choose, adding delicate ones like snow peas just after you remove the curry from the heat.

3 tablespoons vegetable oil
3 tablespoons Red Curry Paste (page 171)
1/2 pound boneless pork or beef, thinly sliced into strips 1 1/2 inches by 3/4 inch
2 cups chicken stock
2 cups water
3 tablespoons fish sauce
1 tablespoon sugar
1/3 cup sliced canned bamboo shoots
1 1/2 cups diced, unpeeled eggplant (1-inch dice)
15 green beans, trimmed and cut into 2-inch lengths
A handful of fresh graprao *basil leaves, or other fresh basil leaves, or fresh mint leaves*
5 fresh red chee fah *chilies sliced on the diagonal into thin ovals, or a handful of long, thin sweet red pepper strips*

In a large saucepan over low heat, warm the oil until hot but not smoking. Add the curry paste. It should just sizzle; if it spits and pops wildly, remove the pan from the heat for a moment. Press and stir the curry paste with a large spoon or spatula to break it up and mash it into the oil. Cook until the curry paste is fragrant, about 3 or 4 minutes.

Add the meat and stir-fry to brown it and coat it with the paste. Cook for about 3 minutes, stirring occasionally, until the meat absorbs most of the paste and oil and becomes shiny.

Add the chicken stock and water and bring the curry to a boil. Add the fish sauce and sugar, then the bamboo shoots, eggplant, and green beans. Return the curry to a boil and simmer until the vegetables are barely done, 3 or 4 minutes. Remove from the heat and stir in the basil and chilies. Let stand for at least 5 to 7 minutes, then taste and adjust the seasoning with fish sauce. Serve hot or warm.

SERVES 6.

MOO PAHT NAW MAI
Pork Stir-Fried with Bamboo Shoots

Bamboo is beloved in Asian kitchens for its crunchy texture and its ability to absorb other flavors. This is a hot one, so don't stint on those chilies. If you like very spicy food, try it with a handful of whole dried red chilies instead of chopped fresh ones.

1 can (14 ounces) whole bamboo shoots, drained, rinsed, and drained again
2 tablespoons vegetable oil
1 tablespoon crushed garlic
About 1/4 cup fresh kii noo *chilies or serrano chilies, stemmed and cut crosswise into small pieces*
1 small onion, thinly sliced lengthwise
1/4 pound pork, cut into thin strips
3 tablespoons fish sauce
1 tablespoon water
1/4 teaspoon freshly ground pepper

Shred or cut the bamboo shoots lengthwise into very thin strips about 2 inches long. You should have about 1 1/2 cups. Set aside.

Heat a wok or large, deep skillet over medium-high heat. Add the oil and swirl to coat the surface. When the oil is hot, drop a piece of the garlic into the pan. If it sizzles immediately, the oil is ready. Add the garlic and stir-fry until golden, about 30 seconds. Add the chilies and onion and stir-fry until the onion begins to wilt, about 1 minute.

Add the pork and stir-fry until it is no longer pink, about 2 minutes. Add the bamboo shoots and toss to heat through and coat with the oil. Add the fish sauce, water, and pepper and continue cooking for about 1 minute more. Remove from the heat and transfer to a serving platter. Serve hot or warm.

SERVES 4.

TOME YUM PLAH DOOK
Hot Sour Catfish Soup

Here is a country-style version of *tome yum,* the classic Thai soup made with shrimp, lemongrass, and lime. This quick, simple *tome yum* uses cherry tomato for an additional sour note. *Plah dook* is catfish, but you can use any firm white fish fillet in this fresh-tasting, sharp soup.

2 large stalks lemongrass
4 cups Basic Chicken Stock (page 186) or other light chicken stock
2 tablespoons fish sauce
2 tablespoons freshly squeezed lime juice
5 small fresh kii noo *chilies, left whole, or 2 fresh serrano chilies, thinly sliced crosswise*
1/4 pound catfish fillet or other meaty white fish fillet, cut crosswise into 2-inch chunks
1/3 cup small fresh button mushrooms, thinly sliced lengthwise
3 green onions, sliced into 1-inch lengths
3 cherry tomatoes, quartered lengthwise

Trim the tops of lemongrass stalks. Cut away and discard the grassy top of each stalk, leaving a stalk about 6 inches long. Cut away any hard root section to leave a clean, smooth, flat base at the root end below the bulb. Remove and discard tough outer leaves. Using the blunt edge of a cleaver or large knife, whack it firmly at 2-inch intervals, rolling it over to bruise the stalk on all sides.

Stem the *kii noo* chilies. Place the chilies under the flat side of a cleaver or chef's knife blade and crush them gently, pressing with the heel of your hand until they split open just enough to reveal their seeds and release their perfume. Set aside.

In a medium saucepan over medium heat, combine the chicken stock and lemongrass. Bring to a boil, then reduce the heat to maintain a simmer and cook for 5 minutes. Meanwhile, combine the lime juice and fish sauce in a serving bowl and set aside.

Remove the lemongrass from the saucepan and discard. Increase the heat to high to return the soup to a vigorous boil. Add the fish pieces and mushrooms. Reduce the heat again to medium and simmer until the fish is opaque and the mushrooms are tender, about 2 minutes.

Add the green onions, chilies, and tomatoes, simmer 1 minute longer, and remove from the heat. Pour the soup into a serving bowl and stir gently to combine with the fish sauce and lime juice. Taste and adjust seasoning with more lime juice and fish sauce if needed. Serve at once.

SERVES 4 TO 6.

NAHM PRIK PLAH TOO
Salty Mackerel Chili Sauce with Raw Vegetables

This chunky sauce is pungent and homey, and when I want a country-style Thai supper I serve it along with jasmine rice, a simple omelet, and a *gaeng jeut,* a mild-flavored soup.

2 tablespoons vegetable oil
4 salted mackerel (plah too)
4 to 6 small, unpeeled shallots, halved lengthwise
6 to 8 small, unpeeled garlic cloves, halved lengthwise
10 fresh red chee fah *chilies*
6 to 8 fresh kii noo *chilies or 3 fresh serrano chilies*
2 cherry tomatoes
1 teaspoon shrimp paste
1 teaspoon fish sauce
1 teaspoon freshly squeezed lime juice
1/2 teaspoon sugar
2 small cucumbers, peeled and sliced on the diagonal into thick ovals
6 green beans, trimmed and halved crosswise
1 wedge green cabbage (about 2 inches wide at the widest part)

In a small skillet over medium heat, heat the oil until very hot. Add the mackerel and cook until brown, about 4 minutes on each side. Remove the fish to paper towels to drain and let cool. Pour off most of the oil in the pan, leaving only a thin film, and return the pan to the heat.

Place the shallots, garlic, chilies, and tomatoes in the hot skillet and brown and wilt over medium heat for 5 minutes. They will sizzle and darken in spots as they cook. Shake the pan now and then to turn the vegetables and cook them fairly evenly. When they are wilted and browned, lower the heat, cover the pan, and continue cooking another 1 or 2 minutes while you fillet the fish.

Break off the heads and remove the spine, other bones, and most of the skin from the fish; reserve all the meat, both dark and light, and set aside. Remove the garlic, shallots, and tomatoes from the skillet and set aside. Add the shrimp paste and cook, turning once, about 2 minutes on each side. Remove the pan from the heat. Peel the shallots and garlic and transfer them to a large, heavy mortar, along with the chilies and shrimp paste. Pound and grind with a pestle to a coarse purée, scraping down the sides with a spoon to mix well.

Break the reserved fish into small chunks and add to the

mortar. Pound again, scraping as needed, until the fish is broken down well. At this point the mixture should resemble tuna fish salad, but be less moist. Add the tomatoes and grind them in gently. Add the fish sauce, lime juice, and sugar, and work them in until the sauce is very moist. Taste and adjust for a pleasing balance of salty, sour, and hot. Transfer to a small bowl, place on a serving platter along with cucumbers, green beans, and cabbage, and serve warm or at room temperature.

SERVES 4 TO 6.

NOTE: In a traditional kitchen, the garlic, shallots, chilies, tomatoes, and shrimp paste would be roasted in the coals of a small charcoal stove. If you'd like to try to make this sauce that way, leave the garlic, shallots, chilies, and tomatoes whole and spear them onto bamboo skewers. Wrap the shrimp paste in a square of aluminum foil or banana leaf. Roast on a charcoal or gas grill until fragrant, softened, and pleasingly burned. You could also use a broiler.

If fresh *chee fah* chilies are unavailable, omit them.

MIANG YUAN
Soft Spring Rolls, Vietnamese Style

Northeastern Thai provinces near the Laotian border usually have small restaurants run by Vietnamese immigrants, and their delicious food is popular with Thais. I enjoyed these delicate spring rolls at Indojeen, a Vietnamese restaurant in the provincial capital of Ubon.

Their Vietnamese name, *goi cuon,* means "salad roll," and that is what they are—a hearty noodle salad wrapped in rice paper. Thais serve them with the same sweet-sour dipping sauce that accompanies Fried Spring Rolls (page 13), but I prefer the simple sauce served in many Vietnamese restaurants in the United States—hoisin sauce sprinkled with ground peanuts and spiked with the fiery Vietnamese chili sauce called *tuong ot toi* or another hot chili sauce.

1 package (1 pound) Vietnamese rice sheets
4 cups cooked somen noodles (see Note)
10 leaves leaf lettuce, cut crosswise into long strips about 1 inch wide
Leaves from 2 bunches fresh mint or fresh basil
Leaves from 1 bunch fresh cilantro
1/2 pound lean pork or chicken meat, poached until tender, drained, and shredded
  into long strips
1/2 pound cooked medium shrimp, peeled, deveined, and halved lengthwise

Arrange a work station where you have easy access to all the ingredients. Have a large cutting board or tray in front of you for wrapping the spring rolls. Next to the cutting board, place a 10-inch skillet or large pie pan filled with very warm water.

Slide 1 sheet of rice paper into the skillet and press gently to submerge it for about 15 seconds. Remove it carefully and place it on the cutting board.

Line up the following ingredients in horizontal rows on the rice paper, starting on the lowest third of the circle and working away from you: a small tangle of noodles, a row of lettuce strips, a row of mint leaves, a row of cilantro leaves, and a row of meat shreds.

Roll wrapper edge nearest you up and over the filling, tucking it under the ingredients and pressing them into a cylinder shape. When you've completely enclosed the filling in one good turn, fold in the right and left sides tightly. Then make another turn and place 2 shrimp halves, pink side down, on the rice sheet just above the cylinder. Now roll it on up and press the seam to close. Set the roll aside to dry, seam side down. Continue filling and rolling the rice paper.

To serve, present the rolls whole, or slice off and discard the ends, cutting each roll in half.

Serves 8 to 10.

NOTE: Keep most of the rice sheets covered while you work with a few, as they dry and curl up quickly when exposed to the air.

These rolls are traditionally filled with a delicate fresh soft rice noodle called *kanome jeen*. Since they must be made fresh daily, they are very difficult to find in the West. The dried Japanese wheat noodle called *somen* is the best substitute and is widely available in Asian markets. Cook them for 3 minutes in boiling water, then drain, rinse in cold water, toss, and set aside. If they become sticky, toss them briefly under cold running water to loosen them again.

MAPRAO GAEO
Sweet Coconut Ribbons

I found this treat in small shops in the charming northeastern town of Nong Khai, across the Mae Kong River from the Laotian capital of Vientiane. Like so many Thai dishes, it originated in China and has been adopted in the neighboring countries of Laos, Cambodia, and Vietnam. Renowned Chinese chef Martin Yan tells me that *yae chee* is the Cantonese name for this wonderful candy, and that it's believed to have the power to sweeten relationships between young and old. That makes it a perfect family cooking project for birthdays and holidays, and that's a plus because opening a coconut is the kind of project that calls for helping hands.

4 cups large, freshly pared coconut meat chunks (page 180)
3/4 cup sugar
1/2 teaspoon salt
1/4 cup water

With a vegetable peeler, shred the coconut meat into very thin ribbons, about 2 inches long. To do this, hold a chunk of meat firmly in one hand and shave strips of coconut from the edge of the chunk. Stop when the peeler gets close to your fingers, putting remaining small chunks aside to grate for another recipe. You should have about 2 cups of nice thin shreds and about 1 cup of small chunks. You could also use a food processor with a slicing disc, although your shreds will be much thicker and less pliable.

Combine the sugar, salt, and water in a heavy-bottomed 2-quart saucepan. Bring to a gentle boil over medium heat. Add the coconut ribbons, reduce the heat to low, and stir to coat the ribbons with syrup. Continue cooking gently, stirring often, for 10 to 15 minutes, as the syrup reduces and thickens.

When the syrup is crystallizing on the sides and forming large, shiny bubbles at the bottom of the pot, stir constantly, using chopsticks or a fork to separate the coconut ribbons a little and to keep them moving. Stir until the syrup dries up completely into dry white grains. Turn the coconut ribbons onto a platter, gently separating them with a fork or chopsticks. You can serve the ribbons as soon as they're cool enough to touch. They'll keep several weeks sealed in a glass jar at room temperature.

MAKES ABOUT 2 CUPS.

NOTE: One hairy, brown fresh coconut will give you 2 to 3 cups of nice ribbons, before the pieces become too tiny to shred. You can grate the remaining cup or so of coconut meat for coconut milk or a coconut dessert, or freeze it to use later. I occasionally find soft, fresh coconut ribbons sold in plastic bags in health food stores, and these work fine.

If the syrup or the coconut ribbons begin to brown while you're cooking them, reduce the heat.

KLAI TAHLAY
The Gulf Coast

Klai tahlay means "by the sea," and all along the coastline Thai cooks use the abundant seafood harvested from the Gulf of Siam in deliciously inspired ways. The Gulf Coast is a tranquil curve of white, palm-fringed beaches, stretching from the Cambodian border at its easternmost point to the Malaysian border at its southernmost tip, studded with charming seaside towns that invite exploration. Culturally these settlements belong in the central and southern Thai regions, but for seafood lovers they're a delectable world apart.

From Songklah, Hua Hin, and Cha-Ahm to Samut Sakohn, Sri Racha, and Rayong, there are a wealth of large, waterside restaurants and tiny, family-run cafes, each serving up the day's catch in deliciously inventive Thai style. Spacious dining pavilions are perched on posts over inland waterways, and simple seafood restaurants lie a stone's throw from the main pier. These seafood specialty houses update their menus hourly as the latest boats chug in, filled with giant prawns, spiny lobsters, *hoy lai* clams, and schools of fantastic fresh fish.

There may or may not be a written menu, but there's never a shortage of expert advice on what to order on a particular day. I loved going with a group of people so we could order dish after dish—a super-spicy shrimp, lime, and chili salad like *plah goong,* and icy cold Singha beer for starters; a seafood *tome yum,* Thailand's volcanic signature soup with lemongrass and roasted chili paste; a platter of *boo jah,* garlicky golden crab cakes served in crab shells and garnished with red chilies and cilantro; *boo ope maw din,* crab claws and prawns baked with bean thread noodles and garlic in a huge Chinese clay pot; and always a whole fish, steamed with lime, chilies, and garlic, or fried crisp and crowned with a dark, luscious sauce of fresh ginger and tamarind.

The great surprise about Thai seafood cuisine is how simple things tend to be. Thai cooks seem to know when to be excessive and when to quit, and what they do with their cornucopia of fresh Gulf Coast seafood is simple: They do as little as possible, letting the natural flavor of the fish or shellfish predominate.

Hoy lai clams are stir-fried with garlic and roasted chili paste until they open and release their flavorful juice, with a flourish of basil and red chilies tossed on as the dish is raced from the wok to your table. Prawns and lobsters are quickly steamed or roasted and served with a simple dip laced with fresh chilies, fish sauce, and lime. Shrimp are tossed into a hot wok with a cilantro-garlic-pepper pesto, and pedestrian fried rice becomes a celestial dinner studded with sweet lumps of crab meat.

You may not be shopping and cooking in a place where shrimp boats bob on the waves with their day's catch fresh in the hold. But *mai pen rai* —"never you mind!" With a little time and a handful of fresh herbs, you can create spectacular seafood dishes with a gloriously Thai touch.

PLAH GOONG
Shrimp with Green Chilies and Lime

Thais don't eat *plah goong* with rice, so it works well as an appetizer. The typical Thai blend of chili-hot, citrus sharp, and salty flavor teases the palate and makes this dish a perfect accompaniment for drinks.

2 tablespoons freshly squeezed lime juice
1 tablespoon fish sauce
1 teaspoon sugar
9 fresh kii noo *chilies left whole, or 1 tablespoon thickly sliced (ovals) fresh*
  serrano chili
1 stalk fresh lemongrass
1 tablespoon thinly sliced shallot (sliced lengthwise)
1/2 pound shrimp, peeled, with tails left on, and deveined
1/2 cup chicken stock or water
A handful of fresh mint leaves
A few leaves Boston lettuce or other leaf lettuce

Combine the lime juice, fish sauce, and sugar in a small bowl. Stir well, dissolving the sugar completely. Taste and adjust the flavor to your liking. Set aside.

Stem the *kii noo* chilies. Place the chilies under the flat side of a cleaver or chef's knife blade and crush them gently, pressing with the heel of your hand until they split open just enough to reveal their seeds and release their perfume. Set aside.

Trim the lemongrass to a smooth, clean, 3-inch stalk, measured from the root end of the bulb. Discard any rough root ends, tops, and dry tough outer leaves. Slice the trimmed stalk crosswise into paper-thin circles, which should reveal purple-edged swirls. Set these aside with the chilies and shallot.

Combine the shrimp and chicken stock in a small skillet. Cook gently over low heat until the shrimp turn pink and are opaque and firm, 1 to 2 minutes. Turn them once, just before they're done. Remove the pan from the heat as the stock starts to boil and scoop the shrimp out with a slotted spoon into a medium bowl.

Add the lime juice mixture, chilies, shallot, and lemongrass to the bowl with the shrimp. Using your hands, mix well. Coax chunks of shallot and lemongrass apart into smaller sections. Stir in most of the mint leaves, reserving a few leaves for garnish.

Arrange the lettuce leaves on a small serving platter. With a slotted spoon, transfer the shrimp mixture to the platter, mounding it on the lettuce. Spoon some of the sauce over the shrimp and garnish with the remaining mint. Serve at once.

SERVES 4.

NOTE: Most shellfish will work in this recipe, as will a combination of several different shellfish. Just cook as gently and briefly as possible, to keep them tender. The lime juice and fish sauce have something of a curing effect, so stop the cooking before the fish is quite done. The wonderful Thai phrase for this is *sook-sook/dip-dip,* dip meaning "raw" and *sook* meaning "cooked."

Any leaf lettuce is nice here, as is watercress, curly endive, or stiff, pale green "feathers" of romaine. Iceberg would do nicely, shredded into a cool, pale nest.

This dish is tasty even without mint or lemongrass, so if they're hard to find you can leave out one or both. Or try it with fresh cilantro.

GOONG OPE MAW DIN
Clay Pot Shrimp with Bean Thread Noodles

The Chinese origin of this dish is evident in the combination of soy sauce, oyster sauce, sesame oil, rice wine, and ginger, and the use of a clay pot, or sandy pot. Its Thai signature is the traditional seasoning trio of cilantro root, garlic, and peppercorns, along with fish sauce. If you like, you can substitute crab claws or meaty chunks of Dungeness crab for all or part of the shrimp. I like to leave the shrimp shells on for extra flavor, so try it that way if you don't mind messy fingers. Don't let the lack of a clay pot deter you. A heavy-bottomed, flameproof casserole with a tight-fitting lid will do just as well.

8 ounces bean thread noodles
2 tablespoons vegetable oil
1/4 cup Cilantro Pesto (page 168)
1 tablespoon finely chopped, peeled fresh ginger
1 pound shrimp, peeled and deveined
1/3 cup coarsely chopped green onion
1/4 cup chicken stock
2 tablespoons fish sauce
1 tablespoon oyster sauce
1 tablespoon Chinese rice wine or dry sherry
1 teaspoon dark soy sauce
1 teaspoon Asian sesame oil
1 teaspoon sugar
1/4 teaspoon salt
A handful of cilantro leaves

Place the noodles in a large bowl and add warm water to cover. Soak the noodles until they become limp and white, about 15 minutes. Drain and set aside. You should have about 5 cups softened noodles.

In a large clay pot or flameproof, heavy-bottomed casserole, heat the oil over medium heat until hot, about 1 minute. Add the pesto and stir-fry until fragrant, about 1 minute, adding a little more oil if it sticks or burns. Add the ginger and shrimp and stir-fry for 1 minute. Toss in the green onion, turning the mixture once more. Transfer the shrimp to a plate and set aside while you prepare the noodles and sauce.

In a small bowl, combine the chicken stock, fish sauce, oyster sauce, rice wine, soy sauce, sesame oil, sugar, and salt; stir to mix well. Place the soaked noodles in the clay pot in which you cooked the shrimp mixture. Scrape the shrimp mixture over the noodles and pour in the chicken stock mixture. Toss the noodles and shrimp a little to combine them with the sauce, then cover the pot tightly.

Place the clay pot over medium heat and cook until the noodles are soft and clear and the shrimp is done, about 10 minutes. Sprinkle with the cilantro leaves and serve at once.

SERVES 6.

AHAHN TAHLAY PAO
Grilled Seafood with Chili Sauce

Try this quick-and-easy Thai way with fresh seafood on an outdoor grill or under a broiler. Have a salad, ice-cold drinks, and plates ready when you start, because this terrific dish will be ready in minutes. The same sparkling sauce is tasty with steamed seafood, too.

1/3 cup fish sauce
1/4 cup freshly squeezed lime juice
2 tablespoons sugar
1 tablespoon finely chopped fresh kii noo *chili or serrano chili*
1 tablespoon finely chopped garlic
4 pounds fresh seafood, such as 2 pounds large shrimp in the shell and 1 pound
 each small clams and mussels, or any combination
A handful of fresh cilantro leaves

Prepare a fire in a charcoal grill or preheat a gas grill or broiler. In a small bowl, combine the fish sauce, lime juice, and sugar and stir well to dissolve the sugar. Add the chili and garlic, and taste. It should be very strong and sharp; adjust the balance of sour, sweet, salty, and hot to your liking and set aside to use as a dipping sauce.

Prepare the seafood, deveining the shrimp if you like but leaving their shells on. Scrub the clam and mussel shells well and debeard the mussels. Place the cleaned seafood on a grill rack over hot coals and grill until done, turning often and taking care not to overcook. Shrimp will curl and become pink and opaque when they're cooked. Clam and mussel shells should open when they're cooked—discard any that don't.

Transfer to a platter and garnish with the cilantro leaves. Serve at once with the dipping sauce, providing forks for extracting clams and mussels.

SERVES 4 TO 6.

NOTE: The sauce doesn't keep well, so try to prepare it within 1 or 2 hours of serving.

PAHT PEHT HOY LAI
Clams Stir-Fried with Roasted Chili Paste and Fresh Basil

Thais make this terrific dish with a delicate clam called *hoy lai,* which has a shiny, beige shell with a dark herringbone pattern. In Thailand it's often sold in kitchen-ready sets, the clams in kilo-sized bags topped with a bunch of *horapah* basil and a handful of red *chee fah* chilies, all ready for this recipe. I've never seen these clams in the West, but any small clam will do.

2 *tablespoons vegetable oil*
1 *tablespoon coarsely chopped garlic*
2 *pounds Manila clams or other small clams, well scrubbed*
2 *tablespoons Roasted Chili Paste (page 177)*
1 *tablespoon fish sauce*
1 *cup fresh* horapah *basil leaves or other fresh basil leaves*
3 *fresh red* chee fah *chilies, stemmed and sliced lengthwise into long strips, or a handful of long, thin sweet red pepper strips*

Heat a wok or large, deep skillet over medium-high heat. Add the oil and swirl to coat the surface. When the oil is very hot drop in a piece of the garlic. If it sizzles immediately, the oil is ready. Add the garlic and stir-fry until golden, about 30 seconds. Add the clams and use a spatula to tumble them a few times in the oil to heat each shell.

After about 2 minutes, add the chili paste and fish sauce. Continue cooking, stirring the clams often as they open and the sauce thickens.

After 3 or 4 minutes, when most of the clams have opened, add the basil to the wok, reserving a few beautiful sprigs for garnish. Toss once to add the flavor of the basil to the clams and remove from the heat. Transfer the clams to a serving platter, discarding any unopened clams. Garnish with chili strips and the reserved basil.

SERVES 4.

NOTE: This recipe can also be made with scallops, squid, or shrimp.

GOONG PAHT NAHM PRIK PAO
Shrimp Stir-Fried in Roasted Chili Paste

Make this quick stir-fry when you're hungry for something red hot. The chili paste is a delicious condiment and is not difficult to make. The oil separates from the paste when it sits, so stir the paste well before you measure it in order to get the flavorful combination this dish needs.

2 tablespoons vegetable oil
1 tablespoon coarsely chopped garlic
1 small sliced onion, thinly sliced lengthwise
2 tablespoons Roasted Chili Paste (page 177)
1/2 pound shrimp, peeled and deveined
1 tablespoon fish sauce

Heat a wok or medium, deep skillet over medium-high heat. Add the oil and swirl to coat the surface. When the oil is very hot, drop a piece of the garlic into the pan. If it sizzles immediately, the oil is ready. Add the garlic and stir-fry until it begins to turn golden, about 15 seconds. Add the onion and stir-fry until it begins to wilt, about 1 minute. Add the roasted chili paste and stir-fry for about 30 seconds. Add the shrimp, tossing them quickly for 30 seconds. Add the fish sauce and continue stir-frying until the shrimp turn pink and are opaque, about 30 seconds. Transfer to a serving platter and serve.

SERVES 4.

NOTE: This recipe works well with other meats or with fresh bean curd and vegetables. Allow additional time for the meat to cook through, and stir the bean curd in gently just before the vegetables are done.

GOONG GRATIEM
Garlic Shrimp

The classic Thai seasoning trio of garlic, cilantro roots, and peppercorns makes this simple, delicious stir-fry a hit with garlic lovers. It might even convert a few nonaficionados to the joys of garlic along the way. Thais make this dish with a lot of oil and enjoy it as a savory sauce for rice, but you could make it with just enough oil to keep everything from sticking or burning and still have a tasty dish.

3 tablespoons vegetable oil
1/2 pound shrimp, peeled and deveined
2 tablespoons Cilantro Pesto (page 168)
1 tablespoon fish sauce
A few fresh cilantro leaves

Heat a wok or medium skillet over medium-high heat. Add the oil and swirl to coat the surface. When the oil is very hot but not smoking, add the shrimp and stir-fry until they begin to color on all sides, about 1 minute. Add the pesto and stir-fry until it coats the shrimp and begins to cook, about 1 minute. Add the fish sauce and toss the shrimp for another 15 seconds to mix it in.

Transfer the shrimp and sauce to a serving platter. Sprinkle with the cilantro leaves and serve.

SERVES 4.

PLAH NOONG MANAO
Steamed Whole Fish with Garlic, Chilies, and Lime

Thais turn delicate steamed fish into an intensely flavored dish. Have rice, other dishes, and fellow diners ready at the table before you serve, because steamed fish waits for no one, at least not with its sublime texture and flavor intact.

1 fish (1 1/2 to 2 pounds), cleaned with head and tail left on 3 tablespoons
  freshly squeezed lime juice
2 tablespoons fish sauce
1 teaspoon sugar
3 tablespoons chopped garlic
2 tablespoons chopped green onion
1 tablespoon chopped fresh kii noo chili

Fill the bottom of a steamer pan or a wok with water and place a steaming rack 1 inch above the water level. Cover the pan and bring the water to a rolling boil over high heat.

Meanwhile, place the fish on a large platter that will fit inside the steaming vessel. When the water is steaming actively, place the fish on the steaming rack, cover, reduce the heat to medium, and steam until the fish is just done through, about 10 minutes. Check the meat near the bone at the thickest part of the fish to be sure it is cooked.

While the fish steams, mix together the lime juice, fish sauce, and sugar in a small bowl and set aside. Combine the garlic, green onion, and chili in another small bowl and set aside as well.

When the fish is done, carefully remove it from the steamer. First sprinkle the garlic-chili mixture over the fish, and then pour the lime juice mixture over it. Serve at once.

SERVES 4 TO 6.

NOTE: You can substitute 1 1/4 pounds firm-fleshed white fish fillet for the whole fish.

PLAH TOTE LAHT NAHM PRIK MAKAHM
Whole Fried Fish with Spicy Tamarind Sauce

The pungent flavor of tamarind adds a sweet-sour note to this rich sauce.

1 cup all-purpose flour
Freshly ground black pepper
1 firm-fleshed round fish, such as pomfret, pompano, red snapper, sea bass, or
  rock cod (1 1/2 to 2 pounds)
1/2 cup vegetable oil
3 tablespoons finely minced garlic
1 tablespoon Red Curry Paste (page 171)
1/2 cup Tamarind Liquid (page 185)
6 tablespoons fish sauce
1/4 cup soy sauce
1/4 cup palm sugar or brown sugar
3 tablespoons thinly sliced green onion (sliced crosswise)
1 tablespoon finely minced fresh ginger
A handful of fresh cilantro leaves
2 small cucumbers, peeled and sliced on the diagonal into thick ovals
10 cherry tomatoes, halved lengthwise

Place the flour on a large platter and season generously with pepper. Using a sharp knife, make three diagonal slashes on each side of the fish in the thickest part of the flesh, cutting all the way to the bone. Dust the fish lightly with the flour and shake off the excess.

Heat a wok or a large, heavy skillet over high heat. Add the oil and heat to 375 °F. Test the temperature by dropping a piece of the garlic into the pan. It should sizzle immediately. Using 2 spatulas, gently slide the fish into the oil. Cook until the first side is crisp and golden brown, about 5 minutes.

Using the 2 spatulas, gently turn the fish over, flipping it away from you and easing it down into the oil. Cook the second side until skin is crisp and golden brown, about 4 minutes. Remove the fish from the pan and drain on paper towels while you prepare the sauce.

Pour off all but 2 tablespoons of the oil from the pan and warm it for 30 seconds over medium heat. Add the garlic and stir-fry for 15 seconds. Add the curry paste and cook, pressing it into the oil until the spices release their scent, about 1 minute. Add the tamarind , fish sauce, soy sauce, and sugar and cook until the sugar dissolves and the sauce thickens slightly, about 1 minute. Stir in the green onion and ginger, reduce the heat, and simmer for 2 minutes. Meanwhile, transfer the fish to a large serving platter.

When the sauce is satiny and slightly thickened, pour it over the fish and garnish with the cilantro, cucumbers, and tomatoes. Serve at once.

SERVES 4 TO 6.

NOTE: Try this spectacular sauce with grilled or broiled fish too, or substitute 1 pound meaty fish fillets for the whole fish, if you like.

For deep-frying, I find an electric wok easiest to work with, because I can set it up away from the crowded stove top and it's firmly balanced on a sturdy base.

BOO JAH
Crab Cakes with Cilantro Pesto

Thai crab cakes are wonderful, seasoned with a garlicky cilantro-pepper pesto and served with a full-flavored garlic sauce or a simple mix of chilies, lime juice, and fish sauce. Fresh crabmeat is ideal, but canned will do. Substitute finely chopped shrimp or slivers of meaty fish for the crabmeat and you'll have tasty shrimp cakes or fish cakes.

Sweet-Hot Garlic Sauce (page 189)
1/2 pound cooked lump crabmeat, picked over for shell fragments
1/2 pound ground pork
2 tablespoons Cilantro Pesto (page 168)
1 egg, beaten
1 tablespoon fish sauce
1 teaspoon soy sauce
1/2 teaspoon salt
1/4 teaspoon sugar
1 cup all-purpose flour
2 tablespoons vegetable oil
A handful of fresh cilantro leaves
3 fresh red chee fah *chilies, cut into long, thin strips, or 9 long, thin sweet red pepper strips*

Prepare the Sweet-Hot Garlic Sauce and pour into a small serving bowl. Let cool to room temperature.

In a medium bowl, gently combine the crabmeat, pork, pesto, egg, fish sauce, soy sauce, salt, and sugar. Mix well, leaving the crabmeat in large chunks if possible. Put the flour on a plate and set this by the stove.

Carefully shape the crab-pork mixture into small cakes. Dip each cake in the flour to coat it lightly. Heat the oil in a large skillet over medium-high heat for 1 minute. Add the crab cakes and sauté, turning once, until golden brown and cooked, about 5 minutes per side. Transfer the cakes to a serving platter and garnish with the cilantro and chili. Serve at once with the dipping sauce.

SERVES 4.

NOTE: In Thailand, *boo jah* is stuffed into cleaned crab shells, steamed until cooked, and then briefly fried to brown the top. If you form the meat mixture into small balls or pack it into tiny cups and steam them, you'll have *mah uan,* or "fat horses," a popular hors d'oeuvre.

Try a simple dipping sauce of 3 tablespoons fish sauce, 3 tablespoons freshly squeezed lime juice, 1 tablespoon sugar, and 1 tablespoon chopped fresh hot chili. Stir to dissolve sugar and serve.

KAO PAHT BOO
Fried Rice with Crabmeat

You can be extravagant and make this dish with fresh crabmeat, or you can be economical and use canned. You could also substitute shrimp, scallops, or squid, remembering to allow enough extra time for any raw seafood to cook through.

3 tablespoons vegetable oil
2 eggs, well beaten
4 cups cold, cooked Jasmine Rice (page 164), preferably chilled
1/4 cup coarsely chopped onion
1/2 pound cooked lump crabmeat (about 1 cup), picked over for shell fragments
2 tablespoons fish sauce, plus fish sauce for serving
3 tablespoons thinly sliced green onion (sliced crosswise)
2 small cucumbers, peeled and sliced on the diagonal into thick ovals
1 lime, cut lengthwise into 6 wedges
Thinly sliced fresh chilies

Heat a wok or large, deep skillet over medium-high heat. Add 1 tablespoon of the oil and swirl to coat the surface. When the oil is hot, add the eggs and tilt the pan to spread them into a thin sheet. Cook until the egg sheet is opaque, golden on the bottom, and almost set on the top, then turn it onto a cutting board. When it is cool enough to handle, slice the sheet into thin threads about 2 inches long; set aside. Prepare the rice by crumbling it with your fingers, breaking up all the lumps into individual grains; set aside.

Reheat the wok over high heat. When it is hot, add the remaining 2 tablespoons oil. When the oil is quite hot, add the chopped onion and stir-fry until softened, 1 minute. Add the rice and cook for 2 minutes, stir-frying to heat the grains and keep them separate.

Add the crabmeat and the 2 tablespoons fish sauce and stir-fry for 1 minute, leaving the meat in lumps as much as possible. Toss in the green onion and egg threads, stir once, and transfer to a serving platter.

Garnish the platter with the cucumber slices and lime wedges. Pour some fish sauce into a small bowl and add the chilies to taste. Serve the rice at once. Let each guest season his or her portion with lime juice and the chili-laced fish sauce.

SERVES 4.

KANOME MAW GAENG
Curry-Pot Custard with Taro and Crispy Shallots

This dessert is a specialty of Petchaburi, a seaside town about two hours south of Bangkok. Most Thai travelers returning to the capital from the delightful beach resort of Hua Hin stop off in Petchaburi to buy some of its justly famous candies and desserts. Anyone who travels that route is expected to bring friends and family a sweet souvenir of the journey.

Kanome means "snack," either savory or sweet, and *maw gaeng* means "curry pot," a mainstay of the Thai kitchen. This sturdy, moist custard, often made with mung beans instead of taro, is cooked briefly in a curry pot on the stove before being baked in a hot oven. The decidedly un-Thai technique suggests a European origin for this dish.

2 pounds taro roots or sweet potatoes
6 eggs
1 1/2 cups coconut cream
1 1/2 cups palm sugar or brown sugar
3 tablespoons vegetable oil
1/4 cup sliced shallot (sliced crosswise)

Preheat the oven to 350°F. Grease an 8- or 9-inch square baking pan lightly with oil. Peel the taro roots and cut into large chunks about 2 inches square. Place in a saucepan with water to cover by about 1 inch. Bring to a boil over high heat, reduce the heat to maintain an active boil, and cook until soft and fork tender, 15 to 20 minutes. Drain off the water and immediately mash the taro into a fairly smooth paste, using a potato masher, a ricer, or a fork. The mixture should be the texture of mashed potatoes; it's fine to have some lumps. Set aside while you prepare the remaining ingredients.

In a large saucepan, beat the eggs well with a fork or whisk, and then beat in the coconut cream. Add the sugar and stir until the sugar is fairly well blended in. Some lumps are acceptable, as they will melt as the mixture cooks. Add the mashed taro and stir well.

Place the saucepan over medium heat and bring the mixture to a gentle boil, stirring frequently to discourage it from sticking and burning. Cook, stirring almost constantly, until any lumps of sugar melt and the mixture thickens a little, about 5 minutes. Pour the taro mixture into the oiled baking pan and place in the preheated oven. Bake for about 30 minutes.

While the custard is baking, heat a small skillet over medium-high heat. Add the oil and when it is very hot, drop a piece of shallot into the pan. If it sizzles immediately, the oil is ready. Add the shallot and fry, stirring and turning frequently to prevent burning. When the shallots are a rich, deep, golden brown, turn off the heat and leave them in the oil to cool.

When the custard is puffed, golden brown, and quite firm at the edges, remove it from the oven and pour the shallots, oil and all, over the top. Place the custard on a wire rack to cool to room temperature. It is fine if the surface of the custard cracks and deflates as it cools. To serve, cut into small squares, to be eaten with a fork or a spoon.

SERVES 8 TO 10.

NOTE: I prefer small taro roots, ranging in size from as small as a walnut to as large as an egg or a fist. But large taro roots will work fine. Peeled and mashed, cooked sweet potatoes make a very good substitute for the taro if it's difficult to find. Also, Thais traditionally use duck eggs, but chicken eggs will do as well. Palm sugar gives this moist, sturdy custard its special deep sweetness, but you can get by using brown sugar.

Thais usually buy *kanome maw gaeng* from a sweets vendor, rather than making it at home, and it's always sold in small square tins. I like to make it in individual servings. I pour the mixture into 8 or 10 greased custard cups, soufflé ramekins, or Pyrex dishes and bake them until they puff up and are browned on the edges and cracked in the center, 15 to 20 minutes. They freeze nicely, but after freezing they taste best if they're reheated up for a few minutes in a warm oven.

BASIC RECIPES

These are recipes you will need to prepare various dishes in this book. There are aromatic curry pastes made of chilies, herbs, and toasted spices; preserved foods such as salty eggs and pickled garlic; and instructions for cooking the very heart of Thai food rice.

Rice is here not because it's merely an accompaniment but because it belongs at the head of every chapter. Rice is synonymous with food in Thailand, and almost everything in this book evolved to go along with it, with the exception of sweets, noodles, and snacks. Thai cooks put the rice on first thing when they begin preparing a meal, and its subtle perfume alerts the family that someone is in the kitchen and it will soon be time to eat.

KAO HOHM MALI
Jasmine Rice

Jasmine rice is a naturally fragrant strain of long grain white rice that is grown in Thailand and is widely available at Asian markets. It emits a subtle, nutty perfume as it cooks, and when I notice that a Thai restaurant serves it here in the West, I always feel I'm in good hands.

2 cups jasmine rice or other long-grain white rice
3 cups cold water

Rinse and drain the rice in cold water to remove starch, talc, and any impurities. Place the drained rice and the water in a heavy-bottomed, 3-quart saucepan with a tight-fitting lid. Bring the rice to an angry boil, uncovered, over high heat.

Stir, reduce the heat to low, cover the rice, and cook for 20 minutes without lifting the lid. Remove the covered saucepan from the heat and let stand for 10 minutes undisturbed.

Remove the lid and stir the rice gently with a fork or rice paddle to fluff and separate the grains. Serve warm.

MAKES ABOUT 5 CUPS; SERVES 4.

NOTE: If your bag of rice says "new crop," it is from this year's harvest and will retain more moisture than older rice. You should use 2 3/4 cups water when cooking it, so it won't be mushy.

KAO NIOW
Sticky Rice

Sticky rice, which is sometimes called glutinous rice or sweet rice, is the daily bread of Laos, and of the millions of Thais of Laotian heritage who live in northern and northeastern Thailand. This chewy, substantial short-grain rice is soaked for several hours or overnight, and then steamed until it is sticky and soft. You eat it with your fingers, starting with a fist-sized portion and pinching off a walnut-sized lump, which you roll into a small ball with one hand. Each bite is paired with a chunk of meat or vegetable, dipped into a pungent sauce, or eaten straight.

For special occasions sticky rice is presented in beautiful handwoven baskets; for everyday meals a family-sized portion is set out on a large plate along with accompanying dishes. Since sticky rice can be served hot, warm, or at room temperature, it's particularly appealing for picnics and outings.

2 cups sticky rice

Soak the sticky rice in cold water to cover by 2 inches for at least 3 hours, or as long as overnight.

Drain the rice and transfer to a traditional bamboo sticky rice steaming basket, or another steaming vessel such as a colander or strainer you can suspend above boiling water. Set aside.

Fill a wok or the bottom of a steamer pan with water. Place a steamer rack or tray about 1 inch or more above the water, cover the steamer, and bring the water to a rolling boil over high heat. Uncover the pan and place the rice-filled steaming basket on the rack over the flowing steam, taking care not to burn your hands. Reduce the heat to maintain a steady flow of steam and cook until the rice swells and glistens and is sticky enough to be squeezed into small lumps, 30 to 45 minutes. Add boiling water to the steamer pan as needed to maintain original level.

As soon as the rice is done, turn it out onto a large tray or baking sheet. Wet a wooden spoon and quickly and gently spread the rice out into a shallow layer to release some of the steam and moisture. As soon as it cools enough to touch, gather the rice gently into a large lump and place it in a sticky rice basket or on a serving plate. Serve hot, warm, or at room temperature.

MAKES ABOUT 5 CUPS; SERVES 4.

NOTE: The cooking time for sticky rice varies according to how long the rice soaks. The longer you soak it, the faster it will cook.

KAO NIOW MUN
Sticky Rice in Sweet-Salty Coconut Cream

Kao niow mun is a luxurious partner to sweet mangoes (page 68), the rich palm sugar custard called *sangkayah* (page 70), and an unusual shrimp and coconut topping called *nah goong* (page 69). This is a simple dish to prepare, but it takes some advance planning. You will need to allow about four hours for soaking and cooking the rice. The coconut sauce is added while the rice is still quite hot, then the rice needs to cool for another half hour or so to absorb the sauce. It is served at room temperature, and will keep several hours.

3 cups hot, cooked Sticky Rice (page 165)
2 cups coconut cream
1 cup sugar
2 teaspoons salt

Prepare the rice. While the rice is steaming, combine the coconut cream, sugar, and salt in a medium saucepan and stir well. Bring to a boil over medium heat, stir well, and remove from the heat.

When the rice is ready—soft, swollen, and shiny, and a bit of it easily forms a small ball—transfer it to a large pot or bowl and pour in the coconut cream mixture. Stir well, cover, and set aside for at least 30 minutes so that the rice absorbs the sauce. Serve at room temperature.

MAKES ABOUT 3 CUPS; SERVES 6.

NOTE: The rice will keep for 6 to 8 hours at room temperature. Do not refrigerate.

KAO KUA
Roasted Rice Powder

In the northeastern region of Thailand known as Issahn, roasted rice powder adds a nutty fragrance and pleasing crunch to many saladlike dishes. Traditionally it's made with sticky rice, but any type of rice will do.

1/4 cup raw sticky rice or any other raw rice

In a small skillet over high heat, dry-fry the raw rice grains until they are a wheaty golden brown, 3 to 5 minutes. Shake the pan back and forth frequently to turn the grains and color them evenly. Remove from the heat and set aside. When the rice is cool, transfer to a jar, seal tightly, and keep at room temperature until needed.

To use in recipes, transfer the roasted rice to a heavy mortar and pound with a pestle to a fine, sandy powder, or grind in a spice grinder.

MAKES ABOUT 1/4 CUP.

NOTE: The nutty flavor and aroma of roasted rice begins to fade once it is ground, so I like to store it whole and grind it as I need it. If you prefer, grind the roasted rice first and store the powder in a tightly sealed jar.

RAHK PAHK CHEE-GRATIEM-PRIK THAI
Cilantro Pesto

This simple combination of three intense Southeast Asian flavors is a classic seasoning of Thai cuisine. Four centuries ago, when Portuguese traders blew in from the New World with the voluptuous chili pepper on board, this pungent pesto was already lighting up traditional Thai dishes. Thai cooks gladly adopted incendiary chili peppers into their culinary fold, but lost no affection for this herb-spice pesto. With chili peppers and shrimp paste, it's the foundation of Thailand's complex curry pastes. Whenever you find it in these recipes, you'll know that Thai people have been enjoying that particular dish for generations. You may find yourself noticing new ways to use it, tossed with hot pasta or new potatoes, stirred into stocks, or dolloped on soups.

1 teaspoon whole white or black peppercorns
2 tablespoons coarsely chopped fresh cilantro roots or leaves and stems
2 tablespoons coarsely chopped garlic

Using a mortar and pestle or a spice grinder, crush or grind the peppercorns to a fine powder. Combine the pepper, cilantro roots, and garlic and work the 3 ingredients into a fairly smooth paste in the mortar or in a small blender or food processor. If you use a blender or food processor, you may need to add a little vegetable oil or water to ease the grinding.

MAKES ABOUT 1/4 CUP.

NOTE: I like to make up an industrial-strength batch to keep on hand. For 1 cup of pesto, increase the measures to 1 tablespoon peppercorns, 1/2 cup cilantro roots, and 1/2 cup garlic.

To keep the pesto for later use, put it in a glass jar, pour a little oil onto the surface to cover it and seal tightly. It will keep nicely for about 1 week in the refrigerator.

KRUENG GAENG KIOW WAHN
Green Curry Paste

This aromatic combination of fresh, hot green chilies, lemongrass, and wild lime peel is worlds better than any store-bought green curry paste. I like to make a large batch and use it within a week or so.

Green curries are volcanic and complex, rich with the voluptuous sweetness of coconut milk. In Thailand, *gaeng kiow wahn (kiow wahn* means "green and sweet") is the curry of choice for the special-occasion feasts prepared for celebrations and ceremonies to which Buddhists monks are invited to bless the gathering. At the same time, the monks earn merit for the hosts by receiving their offerings of food.

1 tablespoon whole coriander seed
1 teaspoon whole cumin seed
5 whole peppercorns
3 stalks fresh lemongrass
1/4 cup coarsely chopped fresh cilantro roots or leaves and stems
1 tablespoon coarsely chopped, peeled fresh galanga or fresh ginger
1 teaspoon finely minced fresh wild or domestic lime peel
3 tablespoons coarsely chopped garlic
2 tablespoons coarsely chopped shallot
1/2 cup fresh green kii noo *chilies, stemmed and coarsely chopped*
1 teaspoon salt
1 teaspoon shrimp paste

Place the coriander seed in a small skillet and dry-fry over medium heat until darkened a little and fragrant, 3 to 5 minutes. Shake the pan now and then to prevent burning. Transfer the coriander seed to a small bowl to cool. Roast the cumin seed in the same way. Combine the roasted spices and the peppercorns and grind to a fine powder, in a mortar with a pestle or in a spice grinder. Set aside.

Trim the lemongrass stalks. Cut away and discard the grassy tops, leaving a stalk about 3 inches long. Cut away any hard root section to leave a clean, smooth, flat base at the root end below the bulb. Remove and discard tough outer leaves. Slice each stalk crosswise very thinly. Finely chop the slices and place in a large, heavy mortar.

Add the cilantro roots, galanga, and lime peel. Pound until the ingredients are broken down, scraping down the sides often with a spoon. Add the garlic and shallot and continue pounding, grinding, and scraping until a moist, fragrant paste forms. Add the chilies and grind them in, being careful to keep the chili paste from splashing. Add the ground spices, salt, and shrimp paste and grind well.

When the paste is fairly smooth, transfer it to a small glass jar, cover tightly, and refrigerate for up to one week.

MAKES ABOUT 1 CUP.

NOTE: It's fine to store a supply of roasted whole spices. Once they're ground, their potency fades, so save that step for when you're ready to cook.

You can use a small blender or food processor to make curry paste. First grind the spices using a spice grinder or small mortar and pestle. Then combine the ground spices with all the other ingredients in a blender or food processor and grind to a paste. Add water as needed to ease the grinding.

KRUENG GAENG PEHT
Red Curry Paste

Dried red chilies are the definitive ingredient of this curry paste. Red curry paste is used as an ingredient in a variety of noncurry dishes as well, including Pork Sautéed in Red Curry Paste (page 27), Red Curry Catfish with Fresh Basil Steamed in Banana Leaves (page 133), and Spicy Minced Pork Sauce with Raw Vegetables (page 81).

1/2 cup small dried red chilies
10 whole peppercorns
1 tablespoon whole coriander seed
1 teaspoon whole cumin seed
4 stalks fresh lemongrass
1 tablespoon coarsely chopped fresh cilantro root or leaves and stems
1 tablespoon finely chopped, peeled fresh galanga or fresh ginger
1 teaspoon minced wild or domestic lime peel
2 tablespoons coarsely chopped garlic
1/4 cup coarsely chopped shallot
1 teaspoon shrimp paste
1 teaspoon salt

Stem the chilies and shake out and discard most of the seeds. Chop coarsely and place in a small bowl. Add warm water to cover and soak for 20 minutes.

Meanwhile, place the coriander seed in a small skillet and dry-fry over medium heat until darkened a little and fragrant, 3 to 5 minutes. Shake the pan now and then to prevent burning. Transfer the coriander seed to a small bowl to cool. Roast the cumin seed in the same way. Combine the roasted spices and whole peppercorns and grind to a fine powder in a mortar with a pestle or in a spice grinder. Set aside.

Trim the lemongrass stalks. Cut away and discard the grassy tops, leaving a stalk about 3 inches long. Cut away any hard root section to leave a clean, smooth, flat base at the root end below the bulb. Remove and discard tough outer leaves. Slice each stalk crosswise very thinly. Finely chop the slices and place in a large, heavy mortar.

Add the cilantro root, galanga, and lime peel. Pound until the ingredients are broken down, scraping down the sides often with a spoon. Add the garlic and shallot and continue pounding, grinding, and scraping until a moist, fragrant paste forms, about 5 minutes.

Drain the chilies and add them to the mortar. Grind them in, being careful to keep the chili paste from splashing. Add the ground spices, shrimp paste, and salt and grind well.

When the paste is fairly smooth, transfer it to a small glass jar, cover tightly, and refrigerate for up to 1 month.

MAKES ABOUT 1 CUP.

NOTE: It's fine to store a supply of roasted whole spices. Once they're ground, their potency fades, so save that step for when you are ready to use them.

You can use a small blender or food processor to make curry paste. First grind the spices using a spice grinder or a small mortar and pestle. Then combine the ground spices with all the other ingredients in a blender or food processor and grind to a paste. Use the chili soaking water as needed to ease the grinding.

KRUENG GAENG KAH-REE
Yellow Curry Paste

Kah-ree is the Thai pronunciation of the Tamil word *kari,* which is transliterated as "curry" in English. This paste will give you the deliciously familiar curry flavors so popular in the West. Milder in chili heat than red or green curry paste, its vivid golden sheen comes from ground turmeric, a cousin of ginger, which lights up curry powder and mustard. Thais love this curry with chicken and potatoes or with shrimp, and either way they add onions galore. The paste keeps well for a month or so.

3 tablespoons small dried red chilies
2 tablespoons whole cumin seed
2 tablespoons whole coriander seed
1 heaping teaspoon ground turmeric
3 stalks fresh lemongrass
1 heaping tablespoon finely chopped, peeled fresh ginger
2 teaspoons salt
1/4 cup coarsely chopped garlic
1/4 cup coarsely chopped shallot
1 teaspoon shrimp paste

Stem the chilies and shake out and discard most of the seeds. Chop coarsely and place in a small bowl. Add warm water to cover and soak for 15 minutes.

Meanwhile, place the coriander seed in a small skillet and dry-fry over medium heat until darkened a little and fragrant, 3 to 5 minutes. Shake the pan now and then to prevent burning. Transfer the coriander seed to a small bowl to cool. Roast the cumin seed in the same way. Combine the roasted spices and grind to a fine powder in a mortar with a pestle or in a spice grinder. Add the turmeric and set aside.

Trim the lemongrass stalks. Cut away and discard the grassy tops, leaving a stalk about 3 inches long. Cut away any hard root section to leave a clean, smooth, flat base at the root end below the bulb. Remove and discard tough outer leaves. Slice each stalk crosswise very thinly. Finely chop the slices and put in a large, heavy mortar.

Add the ginger and pound and grind to break down the fibers of the herbs, about 3 minutes. Drain the chilies and add them to the mortar along with the salt. Continue pounding and grinding, scraping down the sides with a spoon now and then, for 5 minutes. Add the garlic, shallot, ground spices, and shrimp paste, and continue grinding and pounding until you have a fairly smooth, moist paste, about 5 minutes.

Transfer the paste to a small glass jar, cover tightly, and refrigerate for up to 1 month.

MAKES ABOUT 1 CUP.

NOTE: It's fine to store a supply of roasted whole spices. Once they're ground, their potency fades, so save that step for when you're ready to cook.

You can use a small blender or food processor to make curry paste. First grind the spices using a spice grinder or small mortar and pestle. Then combine the ground spices with all the other ingredients in a blender or food processor and grind to a paste. Use the chili soaking water to ease the grinding.

KRUENG GAENG MUSSAMUN
Mussamun Curry Paste

Mussamun curry is a spectacular dish, perfumed with an array of sweet spices that reveal its Indian origin. The number of ingredients is daunting, so make a large batch when you have time and keep it for a day when you long for a grand, exotic feast.

1/3 cup small dried red chilies
2 tablespoons whole cumin seed
1 teaspoon whole coriander seed
1 teaspoon whole peppercorns
1 teaspoon whole cloves
1 teaspoon ground cinnamon
1 teaspoon ground mace
1 teaspoon ground nutmeg
1 teaspoon ground cardamom
3 stalks fresh lemongrass
1 heaping tablespoon finely chopped, peeled fresh galanga or fresh ginger
2 teaspoons salt
1/2 cup coarsely chopped garlic
1/2 cup coarsely chopped shallot or yellow onion
1 tablespoon shrimp paste

Stem the chilies and shake out and discard most of the seeds. Coarsely chop and place in a small bowl. Add warm water to cover and soak for 20 minutes.

Meanwhile, measure out all the spices, combining the whole seeds in one bowl and the ground spices in another. In a small skillet, dry-fry the whole spices over medium heat until darkened a little and fragrant, 3 to 5 minutes. Shake the pan now and then to prevent burning. Transfer the spices to a small bowl to cool. Dry-fry the ground spices in the same way, stirring often, until they darken a little, 2 to 3 minutes. Transfer to a small bowl. Grind the whole spices to a fine powder in a mortar with a pestle or in a spice grinder. Combine with roasted ground spices and set aside.

Trim the lemongrass stalks. Cut away and discard the grassy tops, leaving a stalk about 3 inches long. Cut away any hard root section to leave a clean, smooth, flat base at the root end below the bulb. Remove and discard tough outer leaves. Slice each stalk crosswise very thinly. Finely chop the slices and put in a large, heavy mortar.

Add the galanga and pound and grind for about 3 minutes to break down the fibers of the herbs. Drain the chilies and add them to the mortar with the salt. Continue pounding and grinding, scraping down the sides with a spoon now and then, for 5 minutes. Add the garlic, shallots, roasted spices, and shrimp paste, and continue grinding and pounding until you have a fairly smooth, moist paste, about 5 minutes.

Transfer the paste to a small glass jar, cover tightly, and refrigerate for up to 1 month.

MAKES ABOUT 1 1/2 CUPS.

NOTE: This is a large quantity of paste, so do use a small blender or food processor instead of a mortar if you like. Use the chili soaking water to ease the grinding.

If you're missing 1 or 2 spices, omit or substitute another spice you like. Recipes vary; as long as you have a harmonious and spicy blend, you're on target.

NAHM PRIK PAO
Roasted Chili Paste

This incendiary condiment is the secret to a good *tome yum goong* (Spicy Shrimp and Lemongrass Soup, page 39). It's also wonderful stir-fried with shrimp or chicken (page 153), and for chili lovers it can light up a wokful of fried rice. You can buy it in some Thai markets, or use this recipe to make your own.

Pao means "to burn" or "to roast," and traditionally *nahm prik pao* is made with whole shallots and garlic roasted in the embers of a charcoal fire. For simplicity, this recipe calls for dry-frying the ingredients in a skillet.

1/2 cup small dried red chilies
1/2 cup unpeeled shallots, halved lengthwise
1/4 cup unpeeled garlic cloves, halved lengthwise
1/2 cup vegetable oil

In a wok or small, heavy skillet, dry-fry the chilies over low heat until they darken and become fragrant and brittle, about 5 minutes. Shake the pan and stir frequently as they roast. Remove from the heat and transfer to a small plate to cool.

In the same pan over medium heat, dry-fry the shallots and garlic, turning occasionally, until they are softened, wilted, and blistered, 5 minutes. They should have small, black burnt spots but not be burned all over. Remove from the heat and transfer to a small plate to cool.

Stem the chilies and shake out and discard most of the seeds. Cut the chilies into small pieces. Trim the shallots and garlic, discarding peels and root ends, and cut them into small pieces.

Combine the chilies, garlic, and shallots in a large, heavy mortar. Pound and grind with a pestle until you have a fairly smooth paste, 20 to 30 minutes. Use a spoon to scrape the sides down now and then. Set aside.

In a wok or small, deep skillet over medium heat, warm the oil for 1 minute. Add the paste and cook, stirring occasionally until the paste slowly darkens to a deep brownish black and releases a rich fragrance, about 5 minutes.

Remove from the heat and transfer the chili paste, with its oil, to a jar. Cool to room temperature uncovered, then seal tightly. It will keep at room temperature for 1 month.

MAKES ABOUT 1 1/2 CUPS.

NOTE: If you prefer, combine the chopped chilies, garlic, and shallots in a blender or small food processor with 1/4 cup of vegetable oil and blend to a smooth paste. Add more oil as needed to grind the mixture well. Fry the ground paste in oil as directed in the recipe.

This chili paste can also be seasoned to taste with palm sugar, Tamarind Liquid (page 185), and coarsely ground dried shrimp, and sautéed a little longer. Then it is used as a dipping sauce for fresh vegetables or Crispy Rice Cakes (page 94).

GA-TI
Coconut Cream and Coconut Milk

Like all her Southeast Asian neighbors, Thailand has long found much to love about coconuts. For a variety of savory and sweet dishes, cooks depend on *ga-ti,* a white, faintly sweet liquid extracted from the meat of *maprao gae,* or old coconuts. These are the hard, hairy brown coconuts that are easily found in the West. *Maprao ohn,* or young green coconuts, are seldom used for cooking but are greatly enjoyed as fresh fruit.

Preparing coconut milk requires considerable effort for cooks, so you'd be wise to do it when you have the time and energy for a major kitchen challenge. It's also nice to have someone to help you.

In Thailand most cooks can buy freshly grated coconut from a nearby market. Since that's not an option here, I often use frozen or canned coconut milk when I'm in a hurry, and for most recipes that works just fine. If you take the trouble to open and grate a fresh coconut yourself, you'll understand why any recipe using coconut milk identifies it as a special-occasion dish.

OPENING A COCONUT

To open a fresh coconut, you'll need a hammer or a heavy cleaver, a sturdy vegetable peeler or sharp knife, and several bowls and trays for the coconut in its various stages.

First, crack open the coconut. There'll be quite a mess, so do this outside if possible, or over the sink. Using a hammer, or the dull edge of a heavy cleaver, hold the coconut in one hand and strike it hard, administering mighty blows around its equator, until it cracks and breaks in two, releasing its clear juice.

From this point, there are several ways for home cooks to turn coconut meat into coconut cream and coconut milk. With a small Thai coconut scraper sometimes found in Asian markets, you can scrape out the meat from the two halves. (See Scraping Out Coconut Meat with a Thai Coconut Scraper.)

You can also crack the halves of the hard shell into smaller pieces, pry out the meat, and peel off its thin, brown skin. These pieces of white coconut meat can be grated with a hand grater, and the grated coconut used the same way as the scraped coconut from the Thai coconut scraper. (See Obtaining Peeled White Coconut Meat from the Coconut Halves.)

Another way to proceed is to cut the peeled white chunks into smaller pieces and grind them in a blender with water, using about 1 part water to 2 parts pieces. A food processor will work, but try to use a small one. My large capacity food processor doesn't grind the coconut meat fine enough to yield much milk.

SCRAPING OUT COCONUT MEAT WITH A THAI COCONUT SCRAPER
It is possible to grate the coconut meat right out of the halves of the coconut after you crack it open. But first you will need to find a Southeast Asian–style coconut scraper, a small, wooden-handled tool with a sharp, serrated tin claw attached to one end. The Thai name for this tool is *tii koot maprao*. They are often available in Asian markets catering to Thai, Lao, Cambodian, and Vietnamese immigrants. If you find one of these tools, use it to claw and scrape out the meat, and proceed as directed under Making Coconut Milk and Coconut Cream with Grated or Scraped Coconut.

OBTAINING PEELED WHITE COCONUT MEAT FROM THE COCONUT HALVES
Break the coconut halves into 2 or more smaller pieces with strong blows of the hammer or cleaver. With a dull table knife, pry the white meat out of its hard, hairy shell. Working carefully and slowly, insert the knife between the meat and the shell and move it around, working it in until the white meat breaks away in large chunks. These chunks will still have a thin, brown skin. Don't worry about bits of fiber and shell at this point, because you'll rinse them away once you've finished getting to the white meat and are ready to shred it. Pry out all the white meat and discard the hard, outer shells.

Now pare away the thin, brown skin. I like to use a vegetable peeler, but a sharp paring knife works well too. When you've pared away all the brown skin, rinse the chunks clean. They're ready to be grated on a hand grater for *ga-ti* (coconut cream and coconut milk) chopped for *maprao kua* (toasted coconut) or sliced in thin strips for *maprao gaeo* (Sweet Coconut Ribbons, page 142).

MAKING COCONUT CREAM AND COCONUT MILK WITH SCRAPED OR GRATED COCONUT
The peeled white meat from one hairy brown coconut will yield about 4 cups grated or scraped coconut, which is called *maprao koot*. Place 2 cups of this grated coconut in a medium bowl and add 1 cup warm water. Let stand for 15 to 20 minutes.

Place a fine strainer or cheesecloth over another bowl and squeeze the coconut over the bowl, handful by handful, squeezing very hard to extract as much liquid as possible. Keep the squeezed coconut meat in a separate bowl after you use it. Once you've squeezed all the grated coconut, pour any remaining water through the strainer as well. You will end up with about 1 1/2 cups coconut cream, which is called *hua ga-ti,* the "head of the coconut milk."

Now combine the squeezed coconut with the remaining 2 cups of unsqueezed grated coconut and add 2 1/2 cups warm water. Stir well and let stand for 15 to 20 minutes. Repeat the process of squeezing and straining the coconut. Discard the coconut and reserve the strained liquid. You will end up with about 3 cups coconut milk, which is called *hahng ga-ti,* the "tail of the coconut milk."

Use the coconut cream and coconut milk immediately or cover and chill. Coconut cream and milk are as fragile as dairy products, and will keep for only 1 to 2 days, even chilled. They can be tightly sealed and frozen for 1 to 2 months, however.

One average coconut yields about 4 cups grated or scraped coconut meat, which in turn yields about 1 1/2 cups coconut cream and 3 cups coconut milk.

KAI KEM
Salty Eggs

This Chinese invention is beloved by Thais, who serve salty eggs as a contrast to the incendiary heat of a green chicken curry (page 21) and the blandness of rice soup. *Kai kem* is traditionally made with duck eggs, which are cured for several weeks in a simple salt brine. Once cured, they keep for many months at room temperature, and are boiled when it's time to eat them. Serve the eggs plain or dressed with lime and chilies as in Salty Egg Salad (page 51).

4 cups water
1 cup salt
9 duck eggs or chicken eggs

In a medium saucepan, combine the water and salt and stir well with a large spoon to dissolve some of the salt. Place over medium heat and bring to a boil, stirring frequently. After mixture boils vigorously for about 1 minute, remove from the heat, stir once more, and cool to room temperature.

Gently arrange the eggs in a crock or large jar. Pour the cooled brine over the eggs, making sure they are completely submerged. Cover and keep in a cool place for 1 month.

When you're ready to use the eggs, place the number of eggs you want in a small pan and add cold water to cover. Bring to a boil over medium-high heat. When the water reaches a rolling boil, reduce the heat to low and simmer the eggs for 10 minutes. Remove from the heat and cool to room temperature. Peel and serve.

MAKES 9 EGGS.

NOTE: Salty eggs (sometimes labeled "salted eggs") are sold uncooked in Asian markets. Often they're coated with a 1/4-inch-thick layer of charcoal-colored ash. Carefully rinse the ash off and cook the eggs as directed in this recipe.

GRATIEM DONG
Pickled Garlic

These pickled garlic cloves are a sweet-sour foil for fiery curries or a pungent accent enhancing whole fish steamed with Chinese celery or the dazzling sweet-and-crispy rice noodle dish called *mee grob* (page 58).

10 heads fresh garlic, unpeeled
1/2 cup white vinegar
3/4 cup sugar
1 tablespoon salt

Wash garlic heads in cool water. Trim the stem end without cutting into the cloves and set aside. Combine the vinegar, sugar, and salt in a small saucepan and bring to a rolling boil. Stir and boil for 1 minute. When the sugar and salt are dissolved, reduce the heat and simmer gently until slightly thickened, about 5 minutes. Remove from the heat and cool to room temperature.

Place the garlic in a jar or crock with a tight-fitting lid and pour in the pickling brine to immerse the garlic completely. Seal tightly and store in a cool, dark place for 2 to 3 weeks before using.

MAKES ABOUT 1 QUART.

GRATIEM JIOW
Fried Garlic in Oil

This plain, easy-to-make condiment is magic when poured over Thai noodle dishes and soups. The oil carries the flavor and the golden garlic bits add a soft, toasty crunch. You can fry just enough for a given recipe, or make a larger batch to have handy for sudden culinary inspirations. Making fried garlic perfumes your kitchen wonderfully, and it keeps nicely for 3 to 5 days in the refrigerator in a tightly sealed jar.

1/4 cup vegetable oil
2 tablespoons finely chopped garlic

Heat a small skillet over low heat. Add the oil and heat until very hot. Drop a piece of the garlic into the oil. If it sizzles immediately, the oil is ready. Add all the garlic to the oil and stir to break up any clumps. It should sizzle and bubble and begin to turn golden. As its lovely perfume reaches you, stir gently, and as soon as half of the garlic is a soft, wheaty color, remove the pan from the heat and let the garlic finish cooking in the warm pan. This entire process shouldn't take more than about 3 minutes.

Let cool to room temperature, transfer to a glass jar with a tight lid, and store in the refrigerator.

MAKES ABOUT 1/4 CUP.

NOTE: It's easy to burn this, so be careful. The garlic should be finely chopped, but not minced to a mushy state. If the garlic is too moist it is almost sure to burn.

To make a large batch, simply double the amount of oil and garlic.

NAHM MAKAHM BIAK
Tamarind Liquid

Tamarind liquid is made by soaking tamarind pulp in warm water and then pressing it through a strainer. It has a delicious sour taste, sharp and fruity, like a marriage of raisins and limes. Thais add tamarind to soups, curries, sauces, and sweets for its distinctive sweet-sour punch.

1/4 cup tamarind pulp
1/2 cup warm water

Place the tamarind pulp in a small bowl and add the warm water. Soak for 20 to 30 minutes, poking and mashing occasionally to break the sticky lump into pieces and help it dissolve.

Pour the tamarind and water through a small, fine-mesh strainer into another bowl, and use a spoon to mash the softened pulp against the strainer, extracting as much thick liquid as you can. Scrape off the bottom of the strainer to release the thick purée that accumulates there. Discard the pulp, fibers, and seeds that have collected in the strainer. Thin the extracted tamarind liquid with water until it is the consistency of pea soup.

Use as directed in recipes, or cover and refrigerate for up to 1 day. MAKES ABOUT 3/4 CUP.

NOTE: Thais usually mash the softened tamarind pulp with water and spoon the liquid off the top without actually straining it, but I find straining makes it easier to avoid seeds and fibers.

Tamarind liquid doesn't keep well, sharpening and changing unpleasantly as it sits. I prefer to make it in small batches as I need it and discard it after a day.

NAHM SOOP
Basic Chicken Stock

Homemade chicken stock makes a world of difference in Wonton Soup and in noodle soups.

About 3 pounds chicken wings or very meaty chicken bones
About 1 pound pork neck bones or other meaty pork bones
8 cups water
4 sprigs fresh cilantro with roots attached or a handful of leafy cilantro sprigs
1 teaspoon salt

Combine all of the ingredients in a large saucepan and bring to a rolling boil over medium heat. Occasionally skim off and discard any foam that rises to the top. After about 10 minutes, when there is very little foam rising, reduce the heat to low and simmer the stock for 1 hour without stirring.

Remove from the heat and let cool uncovered and undisturbed. Pour through a fine strainer, leaving the last dregs behind, as they tend to cloud the soup. Discard the bones and dregs.

Cover and chill. Before using, remove the fat that congeals on top of the stock.

MAKES ABOUT 6 CUPS.

NOTE: You can make this stock in quantity and freeze it in 1-quart containers.

For a quick Thai-style stock, combine about 4 cups canned chicken broth with 2 cups water. Simmer with a handful of fresh cilantro leaves and 2 pork chop bones for about 20 minutes.

NAHM CHUAM
Sugar Syrup

Nahm means "liquid" or "juice," and *chuam* means "to candy or preserve in syrup." Thais use *nahm chuam* for sweet snacks such as *som loy gaeo,* oranges and crushed ice floating in a bowl of sugar syrup (page 67). It's also used for sweetening limeade, iced coffee, and tea.

1 cup sugar
1 cup water

Combine the sugar and water in a small saucepan and bring to a rolling boil over high heat. Reduce the heat to maintain an active simmer and cook until liquid has thickened and colored slightly, about five minutes. Remove from the heat and cool to room temperature.

Pour the cooled syrup into a jar with a tight-fitting lid, cover, and store at room temperature for 1 week, or in the refrigerator for several weeks.

MAKES ABOUT 1 1/3 CUPS.

NOTE: When cool, the syrup will be almost as thick as honey. Prepare any amount you like, using equal parts sugar and water.

PRIK DONG NAHM SOM
Chili-Vinegar Sauce

This simple sauce is part of the standard seasonings, or *krueng broong,* found on every table in Thai noodle shops. Its companions are crushed dried red chilies, sugar, ground peanuts, and fish sauce with sliced hot chilies.

1/2 cup white vinegar
1 tablespoon fish sauce
10 fresh hot chilies, thinly sliced crosswise

Combine all of the ingredients in a small bowl. Cover and store at room temperature. This sauce will keep for 2 to 3 weeks.

MAKES ABOUT 1/2 CUP.

NAHM JEEM GRATIEM
Sweet-Hot Garlic Sauce

This delicious sauce is good with crispy spring rolls, as well as other deep-fried foods and grilled or roasted meats.

1 cup sugar
1/2 cup water
1/2 cup white vinegar
2 tablespoons finely minced garlic
1 teaspoon salt
1 tablespoon chili-garlic sauce (tuong or toi *sauce) or coarsely ground dried red chili*

In a small, heavy saucepan, combine the sugar, water, vinegar, garlic, and salt. Bring to a rolling boil over medium heat. Stir to dissolve the sugar and salt and reduce the heat to low. Simmer until the liquid reduces slightly and thickens to a light syrup, 20 minutes. Remove from the heat and stir in the chili garlic sauce. Cool to room temperature.

Transfer the cooled sauce to a tightly sealed jar and store at room temperature for 2 to 3 days.

MAKES ABOUT 1 1/2 CUPS.

NAHM JEEM PLAH PAO UBON
Chili-Garlic Sauce for Fish

Serve this feisty sauce with Grilled Whole Fish with Lemongrass and Graprao Basil (page 131) or any grilled or steamed fish or seafood.

1/3 cup fish sauce
2 tablespoons water
2 tablespoons palm sugar or brown sugar
3 tablespoons freshly squeezed lime juice
1 tablespoon finely minced garlic
1 tablespoon finely chopped green onion
2 teaspoons coarsely ground dried red chili

In a small saucepan over medium heat, combine the fish sauce, water, and palm sugar. Cook gently, stirring occasionally, until the sugar dissolves and the sauce is smooth and slightly thickened. Remove from the heat and stir in the lime juice, garlic, green onion, and chili, mixing well. Taste and adjust seasoning to your liking.

MAKES ABOUT 1/2 CUP.

NAHM JEEM SEUA RONG HAI
Dipping Sauce for Grilled Beef

This fiery sauce is served with Grilled Beef (page 127) and other roasted meats. Small slices of beef are dipped in the sauce, along with bite-sized balls of sticky rice.

5 small dried red chilies
1/4 cup fish sauce
2 tablespoons freshly squeezed lime juice
1 teaspoon palm sugar or sugar
1 teaspoon dark soy sauce
1 tablespoon Roasted Rice Powder (page 167)
2 small green onions, finely minced

In a small skillet, dry-fry the chilies over medium to low heat until they are fragrant and brittle. They should darken and develop small, black spots, but they should not burn completely. Shake the pan to cook them on all sides. Remove from the heat and let cool.

Stem the chilies, cut each chili crosswise into 4 pieces, and place in a mortar. Pound to a coarse powder with a pestle. Seeds and small flecks of chili should still be visible. Set aside.

In a small glass or ceramic bowl, combine the fish sauce, lime juice, sugar, and soy sauce and stir until the sugar is dissolved. Taste and adjust the flavors to your liking. Stir in the green onions, rice powder, and chilies. Divide among small saucers to serve.

MAKES ABOUT 1/3 CUP.

JAEW MAKEUA TEHT
Roasted Tomato, Garlic, and Chili Sauce

This pungent sauce traditionally accompanies the northeastern-style salty, sun-dried beef called *neua kem* (page 128). It is delicious with any grilled meat, however. In Thailand the tomatoes are roasted over charcoal, and the whole, unpeeled garlic and shallots are placed right in the coals.

6 large unpeeled shallots, halved lengthwise
6 large unpeeled garlic cloves, halved lengthwise
9 cherry tomatoes or 4 plum tomatoes, stemmed
6 fresh kii noo *chilies or 3 fresh serrano chilies*
2 teaspoons palm sugar
2 tablespoons fish sauce

Preheat a broiler until it is extremely hot. Spread out the shallots and garlic in a large roasting pan. Put the whole tomatoes and chilies in the pan as well, and place on the center of a rack about 6 to 8 inches under the broiler flame.

Roast for 10 minutes, checking often and turning as the vegetables brown, blister, and blacken in spots. When the shallots and garlic are softened and charred, remove them from the pan and set aside. Let the tomatoes and chilies continue cooking until they are nicely blackened. They may burst open in spots. Remove the tomatoes and chilies and set aside with the shallots and garlic until you can handle them easily.

Peel the shallots and garlic and place them in a large, heavy mortar. Stem the chilies and add them, too. Carefully pound to a fragrant mush. Stop to scrape down the sides with a spoon as needed to mix well. Then add the sugar and grind it in well.

Add the tomatoes, including any juices and skin that stuck to the roasting pan. Carefully grind and scrape the tomatoes into the mixture until all the ingredients are broken down into a coarse purée, about 3 minutes.

Stir in the fish sauce and taste. Add more fish sauce or sugar as needed for a pleasing balance of salty, sweet, and hot.

Transfer the mixture to a small bowl and serve.

MAKES ABOUT 1/3 CUP.

NOTE: The garlic, shallots, chilies, and tomatoes can be roasted over a very hot charcoal fire. Place the tomatoes and chilies on a piece of aluminum foil so you can turn them more easily.

GLOSSARY

BAMBOO SHOOT/NAW MAI

The tender, young shoots of a tenacious grass that grows wild throughout Asia. Pale to bright yellow, the shoots are boiled until tender and then canned. Some are cone shaped, and some have slender tips like asparagus spears. Try to buy whole canned shoots and cut or shred them to the size you want, as the quality of whole shoots seems to be better than sliced shoots. Some Asian markets carry fresh shoots, but they take long cooking before they can be added to stir-fries and curries. Keep leftover shoots refrigerated in water to cover, and change the water every few days.

BANANA LEAVES/BAI GLUAY; BAI TONG

Thais use banana leaves to wrap food for steaming, roasting, and boiling, and as a beautiful tool for food presentation. Buy the leaves frozen in large packages at an Asian market and defrost at room temperature for about 30 minutes before using. The leaves are huge, so carefully unfold the amount you need, wipe clean with a wet cloth, and cut to the size you like. Wrap extra leaves tightly and refreeze. Substitute fresh corn husks or dried corn husks from a Hispanic market, soaking the latter in cold water until pliable.

BANANA PEPPER/PRIK YUAK; PRIK NOOM *(Capsicum annuum)*

Also called Hungarian wax pepper, this pepper is pale green to yellow and sweet to moderately hot. It is used in the northern Thai chili dipping sauce called nahm prik noom (page 83).

BASIL/BAI HORAPAH *(Ocinum basilicum)*; BAI GRAPRAO *(Ocinum sanctum)*; BAI MAENGLUK *(Ocinum carnum)*

See GRAPRAO BASIL, HORAPAH BASIL, MAENGLUK BASIL.

BEAN CURD/DAO HOO

In Thai cooking, fresh bean curd is used especially in soups and Chinese dishes. Usually sold in square or rectangular cakes packed in water and sealed in 1-pound tubs. Sometimes labeled "tofu"; purchase the firm type for use in recipes in this book. Store leftover bean curd covered with water in the refrigerator. Change the water every few days and use bean curd as soon as possible.

BEAN SPROUTS/TUA GNOK

Sprouted from mung beans, these are widely available in supermarkets in the West, but often neglected and allowed to wilt in the produce bin. Look for crisp, firm sprouts with little scent. If beautiful, fresh ones aren't available, omit them.

BEAN THREAD NOODLE/WOON SEN

Made from mung bean flour, these unusual noodles are also called glass noodles, silver noodles, and cellophane noodles. They look like fine wire or fishing line and are about as tough, until they're softened in warm water for about 30 minutes. Then they are limp and ready to be briefly stir-fried or dropped into soups just before serving. They cook quickly, so remember that as soon as they are translucent, they are done. They have no taste, but the soft texture is wonderful and they absorb flavors well. Bean thread noodles look a lot like thin rice noodles, so let the ingredients list on the packet be your guide. It should mention mung beans or even green beans, since the Thai word for mung bean is *tua kiow,* or "green bean." I like big bags of individually wrapped 2-ounce packets, since that's a handy amount and it's almost impossible to break down larger amounts without soaking the whole mass of noodles.

BROWN BEAN SAUCE/DAO JIOW

Sauce made from salted, fermented soybeans. Also called yellow bean sauce. A strong background flavor in many Thai dishes. Available in jars and long-necked bottles.

CARDAMOM/LUKE GRA-WAHN

A fragrant seedpod resembling a tiny head of garlic. Thais use it whole in a few dishes of Indian origin, such as *mussamun* curry (page 175).

CHEE FAH CHILI/PRIK CHEE FAH *(Capsicum annuum)*

See CHILIES.

CHILIES/PRIK *(Capsicum spp.)*

Thais adore hot chilies, both fresh and dried, whole and ground. Chilies contain oils that sting and burn, so cultivate the Thai cook's habit of avoiding touching your eyes and other tender spots after handling them.
    For fresh chilies, use the slender, tiny chilies called *prik kii noo (Capsicum frutescens)* if you can find them in Asian markets. They're often labeled "Thai chilies" or "bird pepper" and are usually sold green,

though they turn orange and red as they ripen. You can use any other hot chili, such as serrano or jalapeño, as an excellent substitute.

Also used frequently in Thai cooking are *chee fah* chilies *(Capsicum annuum),* which are long and slender like fingers, and usually a brilliant shade of red. Though fiery, they are much less hot than *kii noo* chilies, and in most cases are sliced into long ovals and added to Thai dishes as a garnish just before serving. For this reason, strips of red sweet pepper make a good substitute for *chee fah* chilies, which are very difficult to find in the West.

Prik leuang (Capsicum annuum), which means "yellow chili," is a long, slender, mildly hot pepper that is extremely rare even in Thailand. It is used in the southern Thai curry *gaeng leuang* (page 118), along with dried red chilies for heat and turmeric for yellow color. Substitute serrano chilies or omit either type if you cannot find them in Asian markets.

Prik yuak (Capsicum annuum) is a mildly hot chili, pale green to pale yellow in color, 3 to 5 inches long, and fat at the stem and tapering to a point. It is also called *prik noom,* and is used in the northern Thai chili dipping sauce called *nahm prik noom* (page 83). It is difficult to find in Asian markets in the West, but is often found in well-stocked supermarkets under the name "banana pepper" or "Hungarian wax pepper."

For *prik haeng,* or dried red chilies, use any dried red chilies imported from Thailand and sold in plastic bags, or any other dried red chili you like as long as it is hot. For coarsely ground dried red chili, buy it already ground, with seeds and pieces of red pepper still visible, or grind your own. Dried chilies keep for months but not forever, so check carefully now and then to see if you need a new batch.

CHINESE BROCCOLI/PAHK KA-NAH *(Brassica sp.)*

A leafy, dark green vegetable of the cabbage family. When flowering, it has beautiful tiny white blossoms, which are also edible. Thais use it extensively for stir-frying and for combining with noodles. Substitute collard greens, Swiss chard, cabbage, Chinese mustard greens, or any leafy Asian green, or use spinach leaves, adding them toward the end of cooking since they're much more tender.

CHINESE MUSTARD GREEN/PAHK KWAHNG-TOONG *(Brassica sp.)*

A leafy, dark green vegetable of the cabbage family. It often has beautiful tiny yellow flowers, which are also edible. See CHINESE BROCCOLI.

CILANTRO/PAHK CHEE *(Coriandum sativum)*

Also called coriander and Chinese parsley, a beautiful, soft, leafy herb adored by Thais and used extensively for its distinctive flavor and as a garnish. It's often available in supermarkets, as well as in Asian and Hispanic markets.

Cilantro Root/rahk pahk chee

Many countries use cilantro leaves, but only Thais appreciate the unusually fragrant and flavored roots as a component of seasoning pastes. More and more produce vendors are becoming aware of the benefits of leaving the roots intact, since the herb stays fresh much longer with roots. If you can't find cilantro with roots attached, substitute chopped stems with some leaves.

Cloud Ear/heht hoo noo

A thin, black mushroom with no flavor but a pleasing crunch and appearance. Thais use them in a few dishes of Chinese origin. The Thai name means "mouse ear mushroom," since that's what they look like when fresh or when softened. Other common names are *mo-er* mushrooms, tree ears, wood ears, and black fungus. They're seldom available fresh here, but dried ones work fine. They must be softened for 30 minutes in warm water to cover and trimmed of their hard little navels, the spot at which they were attached to the tree or log on which they grew.

Coconut/maprao

Thais use coconuts extensively in cooking, particularly for sweets and to make coconut milk and coconut cream for curries and soups. See page 179 for instructions on opening coconuts and extracting meat.

Coconut Candy/nahm tahn maprao

See Palm Sugar.

Coconut Cream and Coconut Milk/nahm ga-ti

Thais grate the sturdy, white flesh of hairy brown coconuts to make coconut cream and coconut milk. Cream is *hua ga-ti,* or "the head," and milk is *hahng ga-ti,* or "the tail." Canned or frozen coconut milk is a good substitute for freshly made. For coconut cream, stir the contents of a can of coconut milk well and use undiluted. For coconut milk, stir the contents of a can of coconut milk and then dilute it by half with water. It's as perishable as the dairy products it resembles, so keep it chilled and use within 1 or 2 days. See page 179 for more on coconuts.

Coconut Sugar/nahm tahn maprao

See Palm Sugar.

CORIANDER SEED/LUKE PAHK CHEE

The whole seeds of cilantro, also known as coriander and Chinese parsley. Thais toast them in a dry skillet to bring out the flavor and then grind them for use in curry pastes and herb pastes.

CRISP-FRIED PORK SKINS/(KAEP MOO; NAHNG MOO TOTE)

These always accompany two northern Thai dishes, Spicy Minced Pork Sauce with Raw Vegetables (page 81) and Rice Noodles with Spicy Minced Pork Sauce (page 85). The dishes, which originated with the Thai Yai or Shan tribe, have a strong salty flavor for which the airy crunch of crisp-fried pork skins is a pleasing textural foil. Thais buy this snack food in the market, usually unsalted and in 2-inch-by-1-inch chips. Many Asian markets carry them, possibly labeled in Vietnamese as *da heo nau lau.* They're popular in dozens of regional and ethnic cuisines, so look for *chicharrones* in Hispanic markets or cracklings in the Southern United States. The latter two cousins of *kaeb moo* are usually sold salted. Other good substitutes are crispy rice crackers, often found in health food stores; shrimp chips, which are found in Asian markets and must be fried before serving; and unsalted tortilla chips, which provide the mild crunch albeit without the puff of crisp-fried pork skins.

CUCUMBER/TAENG KWAH

Use small pickling cucumbers or large hothouse or Japanese cucumbers if you can. Or use the huge, waxy torpedoes from the grocery store, but peel them well and also scrape out the seeds, as they tend to be large, tough, and bitter.

CUMIN SEED/MEHT YEE-RAH

Used extensively in Thai cooking, usually dry-fried to bring out the flavor and then ground to use in fragrant herb pastes and curry pastes.

CURRY PASTE/KRUENG GAENG

An intensely flavored paste of herbs and spices used to flavor coconut curries, soups, and other dishes. See Basic Recipes for how to make your own or purchase prepared curry pastes in Asian markets. Home-made curry pastes take some time and effort to prepare, but they taste wonderful and keep well. Store-bought curry pastes are a good alternative, and they enable cooks to make tasty curries fast. In my kitchen I greatly enjoy using both. The most common curry pastes are red, made from dried red chilies; green, made from fresh green chilies; *kah-ree,* a red curry paste enhanced with Indian spices and with turmeric for its dusky golden color; and *mussamun,* a rich, mildly hot red curry paste enhanced with cinnamon, cloves, and other spices. Curry pastes come in cans, plastic tubs, and small and large plastic packets.

Dao Jiow

See Brown Bean Sauce.

Dark Soy Sauce/si-yu dahm

Available in bottles in Asian markets, dark soy sauce is valued mostly for the rich, deep color it lends to food and not for its flavor, which is mild.

Dark Sweet Soy Sauce/si-yu wahn

Available in bottles in Thai and Southeast Asian markets, this is a combination of dark soy and molasses, and it's the secret of the delicious rice noodle dish with bok choy and beef on page 54. If unavailable, substitute 2 parts dark soy sauce and 1 part molasses, or even honey.

Dried Red Chili/prik haeng

See Chilies.

Dried Shrimp/goong haeng

Tiny dried, salted shrimp used extensively in Thai cooking. They're quickly boiled in salted water and then sun dried. Thai cooks appreciate dried shrimp not as a substitute for fresh shrimp, but rather as a salty, intense seafood flavoring that stands on its own, somewhat like sun-dried tomatoes in the Italian kitchen. The little crustaceans are more fragile than they look, so buy brightly colored ones in small quantities. Once the package is opened they fade quickly, so transfer them to a tightly sealed jar and refrigerate them, using them as soon as possible. Dried shrimp are sold in small plastic bags, although Chinese specialty markets sometimes carry top-quality dried shrimp loose for sale by weight. In most cases, they needn't be rinsed or soaked before using, since this would leach out their wonderful salty flavor. If they seem too salty to you, use less.

Fermented Soybean Cake/tua nao

A flat, leathery disk of dried, salted soybeans, used only in northern Thailand in much the same way as *dao jiow* and shrimp paste are used in other regions. It is lightly toasted over hot coals and then crumbled into sauces and seasoning pastes. It can also be dry-fried in a skillet for a few minutes on each side or toasted in a toaster oven. In northern Thailand it is sold in small stacks of several dozen, tied with string.

FISH SAUCE/NAHM PLAH

A clear, brown extraction of salted small fish such as anchovies, sold in bottles. It's made in Rayong and other Thai towns near the Gulf of Siam. Fish sauce is the quintessential ingredient of Thai cooking, used to season almost every dish except for sweets. It has a delicious salty flavor, and it is virtually identical to the type used in neighboring Southeast Asian countries, from Vietnam, Laos, and Cambodia to Burma and Malaysia. It has a powerful fishy scent, which fades on cooking, and which Thai food lovers come to adore. There is no substitute, but if you can't obtain it, use a combination of soy sauce and salt to taste.

FRESHLY GROUND PEPPER/PRIK THAI BOHN

Either white or black, freshly ground pepper has so much more flavor and aroma than preground, I hope you'll buy yourself a good pepper mill and try it. Many Thai cooks use preground pepper, however, except in curry pastes, where there are other spices to grind as well. I specify black or white pepper only in some recipes; in others, either would work fine.

GALANGA/KAH *(Alpinia galanga siamensis)*

This first cousin of ginger has a wonderful sharp, lemony taste and a similar hotness. Its Vietnamese name is *rieng,* and it is also known as *galangal,* Java root, Siamese ginger, *laos, lengukual, languas,* and *galingale.* Galanga is pale and creamy, much lighter than ginger, and encircled with thin, dark rings. It's never eaten straight, but rather used in large, thin pieces to flavor soups, stews, and curries, or chopped fine to be pounded up in curry pastes and herb pastes. Frozen or dried galanga pieces make a reasonable alternative if you can't find fresh. You could also substitute fresh ginger, which has a different flavor from its cousin but makes a delicious, herbaceous alternative. Ground dried galanga powder has no taste and no scent, so leave it on the grocer's shelf.

GARLIC/GRATIEM *(Allium sativum)*

Every Thai recipe I was given in Thailand seemed to begin with "*Hohm, gratiem . . .*"—"shallots, garlic . . ."—and it is assumed a good cook knows how much to use and how to cut it up. I had to watch and write it down, so check the recipes for the details, but be sure to look for fresh, shiny heads of garlic that feel heavy in your hand and don't have soft or dusty, moldy cloves. To me there's no substitute for fresh garlic, crushed, peeled, and chopped as I need it. I buy a dozen heads at a time when I find good ones, and keep it handy in a big basket with shallots, plum tomatoes, an onion, a hunk of ginger, and some chilies.

GARLIC, PICKLED/GRATIEM DONG

See PICKLED GARLIC.

GARLIC CHIVES/TONE GOOEY CHAI

These flat green chives have a very strong smell and taste. Traditionally they're used in Thailand's two noodle classics, *paht Thai* (page 51) and *mee grop* (page 58), but green onions make an excellent substitute.

GINGER/KING *(Zingiber officinale)*

A delicious fresh seasoning with an extraordinary flavor, hot and spicy and yet cooling as well. Happily it's now widely available in the West in well-stocked supermarkets as well as Asian markets. Look for shiny, fat lobes that aren't shriveled or wrinkled. Thais don't use ginger as much as they do its cousins galanga, *grachai,* and turmeric, but they like it and it makes a good alternative if the others are hard to come by.

GRACHAI/GRACHAI *(Kaempferia pandurata; Boesenbergia pandurata)*

This ginger cousin is also called *zerumbet, zeodary,* rhizome, camphor root, *kentjur* or *kencur,* and lesser galanga. It has a thin, medium brown skin over a creamy interior and is shaped like a bunch of long, tapered fingers. Like all members of the ginger family, it's widely used in traditional Asian medicine as well as in food. Thais believe it counteracts the strong smell and taste of cooking pork and fish, so it's often called for in such dishes as *moo paht peht* and *plah dook paht peht.* It's sometimes available frozen, which makes an acceptable substitute, as does fresh ginger. Ground dried *grachai,* sometimes labeled "rhizome," is tasteless and scentless, so pass it by.

GRAPRAO BASIL/BAI GRAPRAO *(Ocinum sanctum)*

This is often called holy basil, and it's my favorite member of the herb family to which all mints and basils belong. Although it's not easy to find outside Thailand, Asian markets in the West are gradually beginning to carry it. You're most likely to find *graprao* basil in Asian markets that cater to a Lao, Cambodian, and Thai clientele, and often only during the spring, summer, and early fall months. The leaves of *graprao* basil are not shiny like most basils, nor are they textured like mint. They have a smooth, matte finish and a serrated edge, and the color varies from pure green to a green-reddish-purple mixture, with or without flowers, all depending on the particular variety and the time of year. It's more fragile than other mints and basils, so when you find it, use it fast and use a lot of it. Any variety of fresh basil or mint makes a good substitute; unfortunately, dried mint and basil just don't work—no scent, no flavor.

GREEN ONION/TOHN HOHM *(Allium fistulosom)*

Also called scallions, these are used extensively for flavor and garnish.

HOLY BASIL/BAI GRAPRAO *(Ocinum sanctum)*

See GRAPRAO BASIL.

HORAPAH BASIL/BAI HORAPAH *(Ocinum basilicum)*

The most widely available Asian basil, it's used extensively in Vietnamese cuisine, as well as in the cooking of Cambodia and Laos. It looks and tastes like a basil, with its shiny leaves and anise flavor. It usually has purple stems, sometimes tipped with lovely purple flowers, which are a nice addition to any recipe that calls for the leaves. Thais use *horapah* basil more than the other types of basil, tossing a handful onto curries, soups, and stir-fries just before serving, so that its delicate perfume and flavor are released but not extinguished. *Rau hung* is its Vietnamese name.

HUNGARIAN WAX PEPPER/PRIK YUAK; PRIK NOOM *(Capsicum annuum)*

See BANANA PEPPER, CHILIES.

JASMINE RICE/KAO HOHM MALI

A naturally aromatic, long-grain white rice widely available in Asian markets in the West. Its scent is subtle, somewhere between toasty and nutty, and it's wonderful for general cooking as well as for Thai food. It's sometimes called Thai basmati rice, since basmati is another exotic aromatic, long-grain rice, albeit a bit different in texture, aroma, and taste. I buy jasmine rice in 25-pound sacks since it keeps well and I use it often, but many Asian grocers will break it down into smaller lots for you. The large sacks will usually have been marked "jasmine rice, imported from Thailand" in English, somewhere beneath the brand name and various inscriptions in Vietnamese, Khmer, Chinese characters, and Thai script. See page 164 for instructions on cooking jasmine rice.

KABOCHA PUMPKIN/FAHK TONG *(Curcurbita moschata)*

These chubby, dark green pumpkins are widely available in supermarkets as well as Asian markets. Any winter squash will make a fine substitute, although I think kabocha has an especially sweet, pleasing taste. Sweet potatoes work too, but need less cooking time.

Kii Noo Chili/prik kii noo (Capsicum frutescens)

See Chilies.

Lemongrass/takrai (Cymbopogon citratus)

Lemongrass grows in long, pale green stalks with a woody texture and a lovely lemony scent. It is shaped like a green onion, but is stiff and quite fibrous. Its Vietnamese name is *xah* (pronounced "zah"), and it is also called *serai, sereh, zabalin,* citronella, and fever grass. Thais use only the bulbous base, trimmed of roots and any dry outer leaves. If your lemongrass is fresh, you'll see lovely purple concentric rings inside when you cut it crosswise. Like galanga, lemongrass is seldom eaten because it has such a coarse, fibrous texture and delicate flavor and scent. Instead it is used like bay leaves in Western cooking, to infuse a sauce, a soup, or a curry with its evanescent flavor. It is sliced very thin and then finely chopped before being pounded with other ingredients in curry pastes. Try to do any cutting and pounding of lemongrass at the very last minute, as its delicate perfume and flavor quickly fade away. You'll find dried lemongrass in Asian markets, and I strongly suggest you leave it there; it has no taste and no scent, whether it's chopped or ground to a powder. Soaking it won't help, since there's nothing left once it's dried. If you can't find lemongrass, substitute some juice and zest of lime or lemon. Lemongrass freezes fairly well, so when you find good, fresh stalks, buy an extra dozen or so, trim away the tops, and wrap tightly before freezing. Don't defrost it, but rather use it right from the freezer, about double the amount you would use if it were fresh.

Leuang Chili/prik leuang (Capsicum annuum)

See Chilies.

Lime/manao

Fresh lime juice is a basic ingredient in Thai cooking, but fresh lemons make a good substitute.

Maengluk Basil/bai maengluk (Ocinum carnum)

This basil has a heavenly lemon scent and flavor, and it's used in soups, curries, and noodle dishes, including the northeastern version of *haw moke.* It's difficult to find in the West and it fades quickly, so if you come across some at a market, enjoy it right away. Substitute another fresh basil or mint if you like.

MINT/BAI SARANAE *(Mentha arvensis)*

Thais adore fresh mint, especially in their hearty hot-and-spicy salads called *yums*. Any type of mint will do nicely.

NOOM CHILI/PRIK NOOM *(Capsicum annuum)*

See CHILIES

OIL/NAHM MUN

Thais once used lard for most of their cooking, but today vegetable oil is widely available throughout the kingdom. Because it is less expensive, less time-consuming, and healthier than rendering pork fat, vegetable oil is fast becoming the oil of choice for many Thai cooks. Any vegetable oil will do.

OYSTER MUSHROOM/HEHT NAHNG LOME

Beautiful clusters of dove-gray mushrooms that resemble oysters in both color and shape. They are increasingly available in Asian markets and some supermarkets here. Substitute any fresh mushroom.

PALM SUGAR/NAHM TAHN BEEP, NAHM TAHN MAPRAO

An absolutely delicious, robust sugar made from the fruit of the palmyra palm tree called *toen pahm*, or from the coconut palm, *toen maprao*. *Beep* refers to the tall tin can in which palm sugar is sold in Thailand, so the package doesn't always specify which particular type of sugar is inside. Whether it is labeled palm sugar, coconut sugar, or coconut candy, it's a delicious addition to sauces, curries, and sweets. You can substitute brown sugar or white sugar, or *jaggery* from India.

PEANUT/TUA LISONG

Used more in the south than in other regions. Peanuts are called groundnuts in some Asian cookbooks. Use roasted peanuts, either salted or unsalted, and then salt the dish you're making to taste. Buy small jars and keep them in the freezer, as they quickly go stale.

PEPPER/PRIK THAI

See FRESHLY GROUND PEPPER.

PEPPERCORN/LUKE PRIK THAI *(Piper nigrum)*

The original Thai hot seasoning. Thais use both white and black whole peppercorns, particularly in curry pastes and herb pastes, and ground pepper to season stir-fries, sauces, and soups.

PICKLED GARLIC/GRATIEM DONG

Thais pickle heads of garlic in a simple white vinegar, salt, and sugar brine and use slices or whole cloves as a flavorful foil for sweet dishes like *mee grop* (page 57) or salty ones like *kai kem* (page 182). Pickled garlic is also steamed with whole fish and the celerylike herb called *koon chai.* Pickled garlic is sold in jars in many Asian markets, or you can make your own easily (page 183).

PLAH RAH/PLAH RAH

The strong-flavored fermented fish sauce beloved in the northeastern region of Pahk Issahn. It's often homemade using freshwater fish, such as *plah chone,* layered with rice husks and salt and preserved in glazed jars.

PLAH TOO/PLAH TOO

See SALTED MACKEREL.

POMELO/SOEM-OH

A delicious cousin of grapefruit, it has sturdier, drier flesh and much thicker skin. Unlike grapefruit, it has a round shape that is a trifle irregular, and its ripe meat is much sweeter. Peel off the skin, separate the sections, gently cut them open to extract the glistening juicy flesh, and enjoy it in chunks out of hand. For palace-style presentation to a very important guest, a Thai chef might separate the peeled sections of pomelo into individual teardrops of fruit. Look for it in Asian markets, especially around Chinese New Year in January and February. You can substitute a combination of peeled sections of grapefruit and orange.

RICE/KAO

See JASMINE RICE.

RICE NOODLES/KWAYTIOW

Wonderful white noodles, sold fresh in large, soft sheets folded into packets, or dried, cut into various widths from an angel-hair size *(sen mee)* used for *mee grop* (page 57), to a linguine size *(sen lek)* used for *paht Thai* (page 51), to an inch-wide size, my personal favorite, which one Thai restaurant menu translated perfectly as "big fat noodle" *(sen yai)*. To prepare dried rice noodles for stir-frying, soak them in warm water to cover until they are limp, pliable, and stark white, 15 to 20 minutes. Drain and proceed according to recipe.

RICE PAPER/PAEN MIANG YUAN

Used extensively in Vietnamese cuisine, these paper-thin rounds are softened for making the fresh, soft spring rolls (page 140) that Thais enjoy. Called *banh trang* in Vietnamese, the flat, translucent ivory disks have a basketweave imprint. They are sold in cellophane-wrapped packages, in circles ranging from 6 to 12 inches in diameter, and in triangles of varying sizes. Once opened, they should be kept in an airtight bag or plastic container.

ROASTED CHILI PASTE/NAHM PRIK PAO

A fiercely delicious amalgam of dried roasted chilies, garlic, and shallots. Available in small jars in Asian markets, or you can make your own (page 177).

ROASTED RICE POWDER/KAO KUA PONE

Raw grains of sticky rice are dry-fried until wheaty brown and then ground to a fragrant powder with a pleasing crunch and toasty flavor. A traditional ingredient in the hearty salads of the northeastern region. Either make your own (page 167) or omit it.

SALTED MACKEREL/PLAH TOO

Small mackerel, salted and steamed in Piscean pairs in little round bamboo trays, and sold chilled or frozen in Asian markets. Delicious fried or pounded into *nahm prik* sauces.

SALTY EGG/KAI KEM

Sometimes labeled "salted eggs," a traditional way of preserving duck eggs. Buy in Asian markets and hard cook just before using, or preserve your own (page 182). Salty eggs are often sold covered in a 1/4-inch-thick layer of charcoal gray ash. Soak these in cold water for about 5 minutes and then gently rub off the ash with your fingers under running water.

SATAW BEAN/LUKE SATAW *(Parkia sp.)*

These unique fat beans look a lot like peeled, shelled lima beans or fava beans, but they have a peculiar taste and aroma. Sataw beans are immensely popular in southern Thailand, where they grow on trees in huge, ladderlike pods. Often available frozen in Asian markets, with surprisingly good quality. Or substitute fresh young fava beans, shelled and peeled; fresh lima beans, shelled and peeled, or frozen lima beans, thawed and peeled; fresh sugar snap peas; or fresh snow peas. Nothing tastes quite like sataw beans, though.

SHALLOT/HOHM DAENG OR HOHM LEK *(Allium ascalonicum)*

The first Thai name means "red onion," because the tiny shallots of Thailand have a gorgeous pinkish purple color. Thais also call them *hohm lek,* or "tiny onion," and they use them extensively, usually along with garlic. Look for small, hard, shiny shallots without green shoots. Unfortunately, often the only kind you'll find here are huge, wrinkly shallots with green shoots. But they'll do all right.

SHRIMP, DRIED/GOONG HAENG

See DRIED SHRIMP.

SHRIMP PASTE/GA-PI

A very salty, shrimpy paste of sun-dried, salted shrimp, used in curry pastes, sauces, and soups. Thai shrimp paste comes in small plastic jars and is the consistency and color of thick mud or soft clay. The best quality of shrimp paste is hard to find outside Thailand, so I bring back a supply when I travel there. Shrimp paste has a very strong, fishy flavor and smell, so keep that lid on tight. You can substitute the soft, moist shrimp paste made in Hong Kong, although you should omit instructions to roast or dry-fry it, as it is too soft. *Blachan,* the hard, dry, Malay version, comes in bricks and can be roasted or fried.

SOY SAUCE/SAUS SI-YU

Thais use soy sauce as a background seasoning in many dishes, often for color as well as taste.

SPRING ROLL WRAPPERS/PAEN BOH BIAH

Square, ivory-colored sheets sold in 1-pound packets of about 30 or so 8-inch-square sheets at Asian markets. They are usually sold frozen. Rewrap leftover wrappers airtight and refreeze. The refrigerated kind widely available in supermarkets will do, too.

SRI RACHA SAUCE/SAUS SII-RACHAA

A terrific five-alarm chili sauce made in the seaside town of Sri Racha. Thais love it as an accompaniment to egg dishes and seafood. Disregard designations on the slender bottles that say "mild" and "hot"—they are all very, very hot.

STICKY RICE/KAO NIOW

The daily bread of northeastern and northern Thailand, and of Laos, this opaque, short-grain rice is also called glutinous rice and sweet rice. See page 165 for instructions on cooking sticky rice.

STICKY RICE FLOUR/BAENG KAO NIOW

Used in sweets. Available in boxes and cellophane bags in Asian markets.

STRAW MUSHROOMS/HEHT FAHNG

Available fresh in Thailand. Buy whole, peeled canned ones, or substitute any fresh mushroom.

SWEET SOY SAUCE/SI-YU WAHN

See DARK SWEET SOY SAUCE.

TAMARIND/MAKAHM

The ripe fruit of the tamarind tree, it has a complex, fruity sour taste like a combination of raisins and limes. Buy small blocks of tamarind pulp *(makahm biak)* in Asian markets, soak the pulp in warm water, mash to a thick soft paste, and strain and use liquid. See page 185 for specific directions for extracting the liquid. Thai cooks sometimes use freshly squeezed lime juice or white vinegar as substitutes, and although the flavor is not as wonderful, it will do.

TARO/PEUAK *(Colocasia antiquorum)*

A chubby tuber with fuzzy brown skin, it's something like a potato in appearance and taste. There are many types, ranging in size from as small as a walnut to as large as a coconut. The flesh is ivory to gray and often spiked with purple. In Hawaii it's used for poi, and in Thailand it's used mostly in sweets such as *kanome maw gaeng* (page 160). Since it is peeled and cut into 2-inch chunks before cooking, any variety and size will do for Thai recipes.

THAI COFFEE/O-LIANG POWDER

Roasted sesame seed and corn kernels give this coffee an unusual, wonderful burnt flavor. Thais like their coffee ice cold and sweet with evaporated milk, or hot with sweetened condensed milk.

THAI TEA/CHA THAI

Cinnamon, vanilla, and a little food coloring give this black tea its unusual, pleasing flavor and terra-cotta color. Brewed strong and served only cold and very sweet.

TOFU/DAO HOO

See BEAN CURD.

TUA NAO/TUA NAO

See FERMENTED SOYBEAN CAKE.

TUONG OT TOI SAUCE/SAUS PRIK

An incendiary Vietnamese-style chili sauce, made with fresh hot red chilis, vinegar, garlic, and salt. It is a coarse, thick paste with visible seeds and pulp that is widely available in Asian markets and keeps well. Look for small plastic jars. Substitute a freshly made purée of hot red chilies, garlic, and a little vinegar, salt, and oil, or use any other hot chili sauce such as Tabasco or Sri Racha sauce.

TURMERIC/KAMIN (*Curcuma longa termeric; Curcuma domestica*)

A member of the ginger family, turmeric is an underground stem or rhizome. It grows in clusters of small stubby fingers with a dull, brown skin hiding its gorgeous fluorescent orange meat. It has a faint, earthy taste, but the color is the point here, and it's used in many dishes for that reason, particularly in southern Thailand. Today turmeric gives ballpark mustard and curry powder their characteristic yellow color, and it is found with the ground spices on well-stocked supermarket shelves. It has been used extensively in Asian medicines since ancient times and is the natural dye traditionally used to color the robes of Theravada Buddhist monks. Since color is what matters in cooking with this herb, ground dried turmeric works fine.

Vinegar/nahm som

Thais use plain white vinegar, like the distilled white cider vinegar widely available in grocery stores. Japanese rice vinegar or white wine vinegar will work, though they are more strongly flavored.

Water Spinach/pahk boong *(Ipomoea aquatica)*

Also called swamp cabbage, water convolvulus, long green, and morning glory, its Cantonese name is *ong choy,* its Vietnamese name is *rau muong,* and its Malay name is *kang kong.* It has distinctive hollow stems with widely spaced, arrowhead-shaped leaves. It resembles watercress in color and spacing of the leaves, although water spinach is much larger. Look for huge sheaves that cook down considerably. Substitute spinach, watercress, or Chinese broccoli, adjusting cooking time according to the vegetable you use.

Wild Lime Leaf/bai makroot *(Citrus hystrix)*

Heavenly, gorgeous, emerald-colored leaves of the wild lime tree, used in soups and curries for their unique, citrusy flavor, exquisite aroma, and beauty. Wild lime leaves are also called *djeroek poeroet, limau purut,* and kaffir or keffir lime leaves. They grow attached to each other in pairs. Look for wild lime leaves in small plastic bags in Asian markets, usually in the refrigerator case. They are difficult to find, but well worth the extra effort to track them down. Wrapped and chilled, they will keep 4 or 5 days. Use fresh ones or omit them, as dried ones have only a faint memory of their former greatness. They freeze fairly well, so buy a lot and keep them frozen, using them straight from the freezer. You could also substitute fresh domestic lime or lemon leaves, or a combination of grated lime zest and freshly squeezed lime juice to taste if these little green treasures are unavailable.

Wild Lime Peel/piew makroot *(Citrus hystrix)*

This extremely fragrant, flavorful peel of the wild lime is used in curry pastes. Wild limes, which have a distinctive, knobby texture, are also referred to as kaffir (or keffir) limes. Inside there is only a little rather bitter juice, which has traditionally been used in shampoos and soaps rather than in the kitchen. Wild lime peel is used extensively in Thai cooking. Substitute domestic lime peel instead, or use dried wild lime peel, sold in Asian markets in cellophane packets, and soften it in a little warm water until pliable.

Winged Bean/tua poo

A pale green legume that has 4 sharp-edged fins running lengthwise. The fins seem softly serrated along their edges, as if they have been gathered by a seamstress with a green thumb. According to Elizabeth Schneider in her excellent reference book *Uncommon Fruits and Vegetables,* this delicate tropical vegetable is very nutritious and high in protein, but its fragility in the face of cool temperatures makes it difficult to cultivate outside Southeast Asia and the Pacific Islands. The flavor of the beans is quite mild, but southern Thais adore their starchy or *faht-faht* taste. It is difficult to find them in the West, and they wilt quickly, so keep them wrapped and chilled and use as soon as possible. Green beans look mighty plain by comparison, but they make an excellent substitute.

YELLOW BEAN SAUCE/DAO JIOW KAO

See BROWN BEAN SAUCE.

YUAK CHILI/PRIK YUAK *(Capsicum annuum)*

See CHILIES.

INDEX
(Alphabetical by recipe and ingredient)